Freeing the Heart and Mind

Freeing the Heart and Mind

Part Two: *Chögyal Phagpa on the Buddhist Path*

His Holiness Kyabgon Gongma
Sakya Trichen Rinpoche

Wisdom

Wisdom Publications
199 Elm Street
Somerville, MA 02144 USA
wisdompubs.org

Library of Congress Cataloging-in-Publication Data is available.

ISBN 978-1-61429-484-9
EBOOK ISBN 978-1-61429-507-5

22 21 20 19 18
5 4 3 2 1

Cover photo by Maria Cristina Vanza. Cover design by Jim Zaccaria.
Interior design by Gopa&Ted2.
Set in Diacritical Garamond Premier Pro 11.25/14.56.

Wisdom Publications' books are printed on acid-free paper and meet the guidelines for permanence and durability of the Production Guidelines for Book Longevity of the Council on Library Resources.

This book was produced with environmental mindfulness.
For more information, please visit wisdompubs.org/wisdom-environment.

Printed in the United States of America.

MIX
Paper from responsible sources
FSC
www.fsc.org
FSC® C013483

Please visit fscus.org.

Contents

Preface

Both root texts in this volume were written by Drogön Chögyal Phagpa, a great thirteenth-century master who lived an extraordinary and stainless life near the epicenter of world history. He was the fifth of the five great founders of the Sakya order.

Chögyal Phagpa was ten years old and a novice monk when he accompanied his uncle, the world-famous scholar Sakya Paṇḍita, to the court of Godan Khan, a grandson of Genghis. This was a fate, or an opportunity, that befell many great scholars, artists, writers, and religious teachers from the countries that lay within the ambit of the Mongolian empire. Because of their excellent qualities and through the truth of the Dharma that they spoke, within a short time the two moved from outsider status to positions of great religious authority.

At a young age, Chögyal Phagpa was himself invited to the court of Kublai Khan, another of Genghis's grandsons. He immediately made a powerful impression upon the ruler and quickly became Kublai's favored Buddhist teacher. Chögyal Phagpa's influence and the power of his Dharma teachings converted the Mongols to Buddhism so thoroughly that Mongolia ultimately remains Buddhist in the Tibetan tradition to this day.

By studying the biography of Chögyal Phagpa, we can appreciate the good qualities of the master who wrote these teachings.

A Note on the Text

It is traditional to begin the study of a text by first studying the life of the text's author, and so that is where this book begins. The author of this biography is Jamgön Ameshap Ngawang Kunga Sönam, also known as Sakyapa Ngawang Kunga Sönam, the twenty-eighth throne holder of Sakya. The biography was translated from the collection of biographies in *Sakya Dungrab Chenmo* by Venerable Khenpo Kalsang Gyaltsen and Victoria Huckenpahler. The biography in Tibetan contains a comprehensive list of Chögyal Phagpa's compositions that has been omitted here. Those wishing this information may consult the *Sakya Dungrab Chenmo.*

Parts 2 and 3 are composed of root verses from Drogön Chögyal Phagpa, followed by commentary from His Holiness Kyabgon Gongma Sakya Trichen Rinpoche. The first root text, *A Gift of Dharma to Kublai Khan,* was translated by Acharya Lobsang Jamspal and Acharya Manjusiddhartha (Jared Rhoton) and published by the Victoria Buddhist Dharma Society in 1976. It was revised for inclusion in this volume by DeWayne Dean, with thanks to the Victoria Buddhist Dharma Society. His Holiness's teachings in chapter 3 were given at Tsechen Kunchab Ling, Walden, New York, in April 2014. They were transcribed and edited for publication by DeWayne Dean.

In part 3, the text *A Garland of Jewels* was translated into English in 2009 by His Holiness Kyabgon Gongma Sakya Trichen Rinpoche, Lama Tashi Gyaltsen of Bhutan, and disciples from Singapore, and edited and revised by Chodrungma Kunga Chodron and DeWayne Dean in 2014. His Holiness's teaching in chapter 5 was given at Tsechen Kunchab Ling in 2013.

This book was edited by Venerable Khenpo Kalsang Gyaltsen and Chodrungma Kunga Chodron with the expert assistance of DeWayne Dean, whose many hours of diligent effort prepared the book for publication. We gratefully appreciate the generous offerings of the Hiroshi Sonami Fund, Kirsty Chakravarty, and Jia-Jing Lee, which made this work possible.

Part One

Chögyal Phagpa's Biography

Sakyapa Ngawang Kunga Sönam

1. Holy Biography of Drogön Chögyal Phagpa

Sakyapa Ngawang Kunga Sönam (1597–1659)

Sakya Paṇḍita's younger brother, Sangtsa Sönam Gyaltsen, had five consorts, the first of whom was from Tsanaidap. Her father was Surkhangi Gyatso and her uncle, Shang Gyalwa Pal. Her name was Machig Kunkyi, and her eldest son was Drogön Chögyal Phagpa, born in the Female Wood Sheep Year (1235) on the sixth day of the third month. He was born at Ngamring Lukhung when his father was fifty-two years old.

At the time of Chögyal Phagpa's conception and birth, remarkable signs appeared. Later, while he was still very young, he showed great natural knowledge of reading and writing in diverse scripts without having been taught. He also learned other subjects without difficulty.

From a young age Chögyal Phagpa possessed the supernormal knowledge that recollects former lives. For example, when the time came to determine if he was, as was thought, the reincarnation of a famous teacher known as Satön Ripa, two of Satön's disciples came to see him. Chögyal Phagpa was playing games with other children, but when he saw the two monks approaching, he said to them, "You have come at last." They asked him, "Do you recognize us?" and he replied, "I do," naming each of them. This dispelled their doubts and inspired them with great devotion so that they prostrated to him.

Chögyal Phagpa's father, Sangtsa Sönam Gyaltsen, was a great practitioner of Gaṇapati. At one point Gaṇapati appeared to him and lifted him into space to the height of a mountaintop, saying, "Look below." But Sönam Gyaltsen was afraid. After some time, he looked down and saw the three provinces of Tibet. Gaṇapati said, "Whatever you saw, you will reign over. Because you saw the three Tibetan provinces, your descendants will rule over those lands. But because you did not look down the moment I told you to look, you will not rule them yourself." Then he placed Sönam Gyaltsen on the earth again.

For a long time Sönam Gyaltsen had no sons, and being greatly disappointed he performed special praises to Gaṇapati. At length, Gaṇapati appeared where Satön Ripa was dwelling and said to him, "Sangtsa Sönam Gyaltsen is invoking me with the petition that he should command the three provinces of Tibet. He does not have the karma to rule them himself, no matter which practice he performs. A bodhisattva who has accumulated much merit and is able to dominate the vast world must therefore take birth as his son. You, Satön Ripa, possess these qualities. Please take rebirth as Sangsa's son with the aspiration to help all Tibetan people, including those in the three provinces." Satön Ripa agreed, and in this way he reincarnated as Chögyal Phagpa.

Not long after taking birth, Chögyal Phagpa traveled with Sakya Paṇḍita to Kyidrong. While there, many members of the saṅgha who were disciples of Langripa came to visit him. Among them was a senior monk to whom Chögyal Phagpa said, "My disciple, Tashi Döndrup, is present at this gathering." Tashi Döndrup immediately prostrated before Chögyal Phagpa, shed tears, and grasped his feet, crying, "My teacher still remembers me!" Recognizing that Chögyal Phagpa was his lama from previous lifetimes, he dried his tears and made many prostrations.

At the age of three, Chögyal Phagpa recited the elaborate Hevajra *sādhana* known as Lotus Born from memory. Everyone present was astonished, and they remarked, "There is no doubt that he is a true *phagpa*." From that time on, he was known as Phagpa, which means "Holy Being," and his fame was widely proclaimed.

At the age of eight, Chögyal Phagpa recited the Buddha's life story. At the age of nine, while his uncle, Sakya Paṇḍita, was turning the wheel of the Dharma, Chögyal Phagpa recited the second chapter of the Hevajra root tantra from memory. He also gave a profound talk at a Dharma gathering. Many scholars and other learned ones were present, yet everyone without exception was humbled by his knowledge and praised his natural good qualities and wisdom.

At the age of ten, Chögyal Phagpa journeyed to the north of Sakya where Sakya Paṇḍita was the abbot and master of ceremonies, and from him Chögyal Phagpa received novice ordination. Then he received instructions in the *vinaya* from the abbot of the Kyormo lungpa, Sherab Sengé.

By the time Chögyal Phagpa was seventeen, Sakya Paṇḍita had transferred to him all his teachings, his responsibilities, and also his good qualities, and he was very pleased with him. Seeing that Chögyal Phagpa had the ability to carry on his holy activities, Sakya Paṇḍita gave him his conch shell, his alms bowl, and other religious objects. He also gave him the responsibility of leading his disciples, saying, "Now it is time for you to carry on the holy activities of spreading Lord Buddha's doctrine and working for the benefit of all sentient beings. Know that you made this commitment in previous lives." So saying, Sakya Paṇḍita transferred to Chögyal Phagpa responsibility for maintaining the doctrine.

In the Year of the Ox (1253), Kublai Khan, the emperor of China, invited Chögyal Phagpa to his palace. The emperor asked him many questions that others could not answer to his satisfaction, and Chögyal Phagpa responded with such logic and reasoning that the emperor was pleased. Then Kublai Khan said, "Tell me, who are considered greatest among Tibetans?" Chögyal Phagpa replied, "In Tibet, the greatest are the three Dharma rulers."

The emperor asked, "Why do you say they are the greatest?" Chögyal Phagpa replied, "Songtsen Gampo was an emanation of Avalokiteśvara, the bodhisattva of compassion; Trisong Detsen was an emanation of Mañjuśrī, the bodhisattva of wisdom; and Tri Ralpachen was an emanation of Vajrapāṇi, the bodhisattva of spiritual power. This is why we consider them to be the three greatest."

Kublai Khan continued, "Who is considered the bravest in Tibet?" Chögyal Phagpa replied, "Milarepa." "Why so?" asked the emperor. Chögyal Phagpa replied, "Because early in his life he subjugated his enemies, but later he entered into the spiritual path and practiced the Dharma, through which he reached the highest attainment. Both these activities he accomplished within one lifetime. Therefore we consider him to be Tibet's bravest person."

Then the emperor asked, "Who is Tibet's most learned person?" Chögyal Phagpa replied, "The most learned person is my teacher, Sakya Paṇḍita."

Kublai Khan pursued the question. "How learned is he? Tell me of his good qualities and how much you learned from him." Chögyal Phagpa replied, "Sakya Paṇḍita's knowledge is like the ocean. What I received from him is but a small measure of water from that ocean."

Later, the emperor proclaimed that he would send tax collectors to Tibet and draft its people into his armies. Chögyal Phagpa urged the emperor many times against this plan, saying, "Tibet is a small country and far to the west. It hasn't much land, lacks material wealth, and the population is sparse. The country is unable to sustain taxes, and it does not have people enough to man your armies. I beg you not to require this of them." But the emperor was adamant, and Chögyal Phagpa became discouraged.

"In that case," Chögyal Phagpa said, "since I, a Tibetan Buddhist monk, am here as your guest, there is no more reason for me to remain. I shall prepare to return to my own land." The emperor said, "Very well, go if you wish." But Kublai Khan's wife, Empress Chabi, said, "We cannot find a Dharma teacher anywhere like Chögyal Phagpa. The previous masters who have come, Tsalpa and the rest, have not even a small portion of Chögyal Phagpa's good qualities, nor have they performed such wonderful deeds. It is not wise to let him return to Tibet. You should discuss the Dharma with him further and come to learn more of his good qualities."

The emperor followed her suggestion and engaged Chögyal Phagpa in Dharma discussions. During one of these, Chögyal Phagpa manifested an attitude of pride. Kublai Khan asked, "Why are you arrogant? What good qualities do you have?" Chögyal Phagpa said, "I do not have much ability. However, we Sakyapa have some higher accomplishments through our Dharma connections with the kings of Tibet, and through the teacher-disciple relationship that Tibetan masters have had with India, China, Minyak, and the Mön."

Kublai Khan replied sharply, "Monk, do not tell me lies. When were the regions of Tibet under one king, and when did he rule? You are telling untruths that discredit your position as a monk." Chögyal Phagpa replied, "I do not lie. Tibet has had a number of kings who, moreover, fought against China and captured two-thirds of that region, and the population became their subjects. After this, the rulers of Tibet and China established harmonious relations through royal marriages. A Chinese princess was sent to Tibet, and the Jowo Śākyamuni statue was offered to Tibet for its national shrine. These are true events." "If what you say is true," Kublai Khan replied, "there should be records of these things in my imperial library." Then he commanded an attendant to consult the historical records, and in this way he found that everything Chögyal Phagpa had said was true.

The emperor was gratified by Chögyal Phagpa's knowledge. Then Chögyal Phagpa told Kublai Khan, "These things, being recent, are not difficult to check in the histories. But a million years previously, there was a rain of blood here. This will also be discovered in the records." The emperor consulted the histories and found to his satisfaction that this also was true. Chögyal Phagpa further informed Kublai Khan, "In previous times, the ancestors of my lineage were venerated by the kings of Minyak. They were offered a silk brocade canopy ornamented with deer horn as a symbol of the teacher-disciple connection between our lineage and the kings of Minyak." Kublai Khan then sent emissaries to the Sakya to ascertain if what Chögyal Phagpa had said was true. The canopy was found exactly as Chögyal Phagpa had described.

At length, Kublai Khan developed deep respect for Chögyal Phagpa, and the empress said to her husband, "Isn't it wise that we didn't let Chögyal Phagpa return to Tibet? We should receive teachings from him. I have heard that the Sakyapa have unique Vajrayāna empowerments not possessed by the other schools. We must ask him to give us these." The emperor replied, "You take the empowerments first. If they prove worthwhile, then I will take them also."

The empress went to Chögyal Phagpa and requested the Hevajra empowerment. She asked, "What special offering should I make for this empowerment?" Chögyal Phagpa replied, "As a sign of appreciation for receiving this empowerment, one should offer one's physical body, material goods, and other possessions, especially anything to which one is strongly attached. These are appropriate tokens of one's appreciation."

The empress said, "When I came to the court, my family gave me these earrings, the most valuable part of my dowry. I never remove them from my ears, but I will now offer one to you." So saying, she removed a large pearl from her ear and offered it to Chögyal Phagpa. Later, he sold it to a

Mongolian merchant for a large measure of gold and one thousand measures of silver. When he returned to Tibet, he offered a portion of this wealth to a large gathering of the saṅgha at Tsang Chumik Ringmo, and with the remainder, he built a golden pagoda upon the Sakya Monastery.

After the empress received the Hevajra empowerment, she told Kublai Khan, "The Dharma that I received is truly profound and extraordinary. You should receive it, too." The emperor then requested that Chögyal Phagpa give him the empowerment. Chögyal Phagpa replied, "You will probably not be able to preserve the *samaya* that must be taken with this empowerment, and furthermore we do not have a translator. However, I will consider your request at another time when the proper conditions are assembled." The emperor asked, "What kind of samaya must I observe?" Chögyal Phagpa replied, "After receiving an empowerment, one should venerate the guru who bestowed it and seat him on a throne higher than one's own. With one's body, one must prostrate to him; with one's voice, one should follow whatever instructions he gives; and with one's mind, one should not go against the lama's intent. You may not be able to do these things."

Then the empress offered a compromise. "When the emperor receives the empowerments with a small gathering of his inner circle, he will seat the lama on a throne higher than his, but when there are public gatherings with palace dignitaries, their retinues, and other important persons, the emperor will sit upon the highest throne to preserve the hierarchical tradition. Regarding activities related to Tibet, the emperor should not give orders to the Tibetans without first consulting the lama. Regarding other matters, they should be made by the emperor in consultation with the lama because the lama has the nature of great compassion. However, because some people might take unfair advantage of the lama's kindness, he, in turn, should confer on all decisions with the emperor." Chögyal Phagpa agreed to these conditions.

Then Chögyal Phagpa told Kublai Khan, "In the Mongolian tradition, you would not promote a member of the military to a higher rank until he had successfully entered the field of battle. Likewise, according to our tradition, the teacher performs a deity retreat before bestowing a higher empowerment upon his students. I must therefore do a retreat before giving you the empowerment." So saying, Chögyal Phagpa entered retreat. Meanwhile, the emperor sent messengers in all directions to summon a learned translator to the palace. Then Chögyal Phagpa bestowed on the emperor of China and twenty-four members of his retinue the complete Śrī Hevajra empowerment, which is unique to the Sakya tradition. In this way, the Vajrayāna began to be established in the lands of China and Mongolia.

To show his appreciation for receiving this empowerment, the emperor made Chögyal Phagpa an offering of thirteen groups of ten thousand subjects each. One group of ten thousand is called a *trikor*. Within one trikor are four thousand religious communities and six thousand lay families. The emperor's second offering consisted of a conch shell known as the "holy white conch shell."

He also offered Chögyal Phagpa authority over the religious communities and the lay inhabitants of the three provinces of Tibet. The three provinces of Tibet comprised the following: the territory from the three Ngari regions of western Tibet to Sokla Kyapo, known as the "Holy Dharma Province"; the territory from Sokla Kyapo down to the Machu River, known as the "Human Province"; and the territory from the Machu River to the "White Stūpa of China," known as the "Horse Province."

During Kublai Khan's reign, his kingdom encompassed eleven *shing* and the three provinces given to Chögyal Phagpa were counted as one shing. In reality, the three did not have enough inhabitants to qualify as a shing, but since it was the land where the emperor's teacher resided, and since it was a place where the Dharma was widely practiced, it was allowed to be counted as one shing.

At that time, the Chinese empire was divided in the following way: a family unit for official purposes included a structure containing six pillars that housed the six elements of a family—the husband, the wife, the sons, the daughters, and the male and female servants. These, together with domestic animals such as horses, donkeys, cows, and sheep, and such lands as would yield twelve loads of grain, were counted as one simple, single family. Twenty-five of these made one community. Two communities were known as one *tago*. Two tago constituted one hundred family circles. Ten times one hundred family circles constituted one thousand circles. Ten times one thousand circles constituted one trikor; ten trikor were one *lu*; and ten lu were one shing.

For the third empowerment, Chögyal Phagpa requested that the emperor cease executing Chinese people by drowning. By requesting a cessation of this policy, Chögyal Phagpa saved thousands of lives. This offering was particularly pleasing to Chögyal Phagpa, and he composed the following song of appreciation:

> The elements of the sky are as red as blood.
> The corpses of the flat-footed ones fill the oceans.
> I dedicate the merit of
> The virtue of stopping such acts:
> May the intentions of the lord of wisdom be fulfilled;
> May the doctrine of benefit and happiness constantly flourish;
> And may the lord of nations live long.

The History of the White Conch Shell Offered as a Token for the Second Empowerment

> The famous white conch shell with the melody of Brahmā,
> Came from the crown of the glorious king of nāgas.
> When Lord Buddha turned the wheel of Dharma,
> It was offered to him by Indra.

As this verse explains, when the perfect and fully enlightened Buddha turned the wheel of Dharma, the white conch shell, which is an authentic relic from an unmistaken source and full of blessings, was used as a summons to the turning of the wheel of Dharma.

During the reign of the Indian King Dharmapāla, there lived a Chinese king known as Devarāja ("King of the Gods"). Though the two never met, they became friendly through the exchange of letters. At that time, heretic armies destroyed the university of Nālandā, as well as much of the Buddhist doctrine in India. Dharmapāla requested that the Chinese king send troops to help him. The Chinese king said that although sending troops would not be possible, he would support him with supplies, and he sent a great quantity of supplies to Dharmapāla. Through this assistance, the Indian king defeated the heretics.

Devarāja encouraged Dharmapāla to reestablish the Buddhist doctrine and not permit it to decline. To this end, he pledged his support and sent further gifts, among which was a robe constructed entirely without seams, which was proof against all manner of weapons. At the place of the heart, the robe was sewn with precious pearls. Devarāja also sent much helpful advice through which King Dharmapāla prevailed in battle and reestablished the Buddhist doctrine. In gratitude, Dharmapāla sent a letter to Devarāja thanking him for his kindness and support, and offering to send any gifts that the Chinese king might request.

Devarāja replied to the Indian king, "If you truly wish to send me gifts, I would like to have the statue of the eight-year-old Buddha, the conch shell for summoning the assembly, and the following texts: the *Riverbank Sūtra*, the *Gaṇḍavyūha Sūtra*, the *Treasury of Vinaya*, and the *Kāraṇḍavyūha Sūtra*. I also wish you to send four fully ordained monks with pure discipline."

The Indian king replied, "The statue of which you speak sits on my personal shrine, and although I have strong attachment to it and do not wish to give it away, because of your kindness and goodwill, I shall not refuse. Having received it, please perform beneficial actions for all living beings." So saying, he sent many other material offerings, including statues, the white conch shell for summoning the assembly, and the sūtras that were requested.

As described above, this shell, which was used to summon gatherings during the turning of the wheel of Dharma in China, was offered to Chögyal Phagpa by Kublai Khan at the time of the Hevajra empowerment. Another source states that the shell was offered by Godan Khan to Sakya Paṇḍita, who then gave it to Chögyal Phagpa. However, both sources agree that the shell was used by Sakya Paṇḍita at a special Dharma gathering in which he gave teachings in the Mongolian language as well as in many Chinese dialects, thus widely spreading the doctrine of Lord Buddha to many people.

In this way, the special Dharma conch shell of the perfectly and fully enlightened Buddha Śākyamuni was brought from China to the Sakya

Monastery by Chögyal Phagpa, and it resides there as an excellent, holy object of veneration for countless living beings. The positive qualities of the holy Dharma conch cannot be fully described, but in brief, when those beings having few karmic obscurations look upon this shell, they can see upon it many naturally arisen designs such as the Kālacakra mantra. The sound of the shell purifies the obscurations of negative deeds accumulated through millions of eons, closes the door to lower rebirth, places beings in a state of liberation, and brings happiness and joy to all. It calms wrathful spirits, and its sound mitigates natural disasters such as hail storms. It also brings happiness and prosperity to all sentient beings dwelling in that region.

Chögyal Phagpa's Display of Accomplishment

The Dharma king, Chögyal Phagpa, was venerated by the emperor as a supreme teacher and was awarded the title *tishri* (teacher of the emperor). At that time, certain other Tibetan masters such as the great master Karma Pakshi were visiting China and demonstrating miraculous abilities. In response to this, the emperor declared before the empress, ministers, and other dignitaries, "Our great teacher is none other than the Buddha Amitābha in human form. In reality, there is no difference between his accomplishments and those of previous masters insofar as miraculous abilities are concerned. However, from ordinary beings' perspectives, saints with thick beards [referring to Karma Pakshi] appear to perform the most amazing marvels."

The Empress Chabi maintained unshakable faith in Chögyal Phagpa and in the Sakya doctrine. While visiting Chögyal Phagpa one day, she told him of the emperor's remark and made the following request: "Rinpoche, in order to make firm the emperor's faith, please perform a miraculous feat. Unless you do so, there is the risk that his trust and confidence will falter."

Chögyal Phagpa replied, "The great Karma Pakshi [the second Karmapa] performed wonders and tamed those beings that needed it because he is a well-accomplished master. I rejoice in what he did. Nevertheless, if it will help the emperor establish solid faith and maintain the samaya, then I will grant your request. In the Vajrayāna it is said that if at a crucial moment a teacher fails to fulfill the wishes of his student, he is committing a great fault. Therefore bring me a sharp sword from the armory and ask the emperor and his ministers to come and watch." The empress did as he requested.

When they had gathered, Chögyal Phagpa addressed the assembly: "Now I will bless my limbs as the five *dhyani* buddhas. All of you who are assembled here, make aspiration prayers to be reborn in whichever pure realm you wish." So saying, Chögyal Phagpa cut off his head, arms, and legs. These were transformed into four dhyani buddhas while his head become Mahāvairocana. Then the emperor, empress, and ministers performed prostrations and circumambulations, and they made aspirations, each according to their capacity.

While performing circumambulations, they saw that Chögyal Phagpa's torso, which was still on the throne, was bleeding. Seeing this, the emperor and ministers cried out and begged that he return to his former shape, but for a long time Chögyal Phagpa did not respond to them. Finally, the Empress Chabi begged him, "Protector of the world, please reverse this wonder as soon as possible. If you do not, the emperor may have a heart attack." At her request, Chögyal Phagpa reappeared in the form of a lama as before.

Later, when many great scholars and well-accomplished *mahāsiddhas* visited China and performed various miracles, the emperor thought, "Though these are amazing demonstrations and of great benefit to sentient beings, no one can exceed the good qualities manifested by the great teacher, Chögyal Phagpa." From that day forward, he had no further doubts regarding Chögyal Phagpa's realization.

When Chögyal Phagpa was nineteen years old, he bestowed an empowerment upon Kublai Khan during the new year celebration of the Female Water Ox Year (1253). It was at this time that the emperor offered his teacher the title of tishri. He also offered Chögyal Phagpa a seal made of jade that bore the letter *SA* with designs of jewels. Additionally, he offered gold, a Dharma robe adorned with pearls, a hood, shoes, a golden throne, a canopy, a tea set, and camels and mules bearing saddles decorated with gold. He also offered Chögyal Phagpa the subjects, provinces, and conch shell described above.

The following year, the Year of the Tiger (1254), the emperor issued the decree called Strengthening Buddhism, also known as the Tibetan Script Decree. On that occasion, he offered Chögyal Phagpa fifty-six large measures of silver coins, two hundred bricks of tea, eighty bolts of silk brocade, and one thousand bolts of other fabrics. In addition, the emperor agreed to Chögyal Phagpa's request that the Chinese no longer demand that their emissaries and messengers visiting Tibet be lodged in private homes, or make private citizens responsible for their board and transport. He also agreed to cease imposing taxes on the Tibetans. The decree stated: "In the west of China, the Buddhist religion shall be practiced under the leadership of the Sakyapa."

At one point the emperor told Chögyal Phagpa, "All Tibetans should follow the Sakyapa tradition. No other sect should prevail. Let us make this a rule." To which Chögyal Phagpa replied, "We must help beings to follow Buddhism, each according to his own tradition. It is not proper to forcibly convert beings." The emperor and his teacher determined that those traditions that already existed should continue in their own way. Thus both the emperor and teacher demonstrated compassion and proper use of authority. Through the kindness and accomplishments of Chögyal Phagpa, all living beings in the region north of the Land of Snows found peace and happiness.

In order to help the Tibetans live according to the rule of law, the emperor wrote two decrees, the Pearl-like Decree and Strengthening Buddhism, or the Tibetan Script Decree, and these can be found in the text *Sakya Dungrab*.

The Dharma lord, Chögyal Phagpa, the teacher who brought benefit and peace to many parts of the world and especially to Tibet, taught the Dharma in many languages and spread the Buddhist doctrine widely. He had, in fact, been prophesied by Guru Rinpoche (Padmasambhava), who, during the reign of King Trisong Detsen, said:

> You, the translator Kawa Paltsek,
> Will benefit beings in India and China.
> Then you will associate with me, Padmasambhava, in Oḍḍiyāna,
> And will appear in the Khon family
> In the Sheep Year, at the place known as Trompa in Tsang,

> And with the name of Chögyal Phagpa,
> Will uphold the doctrines of the Tripiṭaka and Mantra
> And tame the savages.

Chögyal Phagpa performed these activities as prophesied.

The following year, the emperor left to engage in battle in the land of Jang (Yunan Province). During this time, Chögyal Phagpa traveled in the north, where he consecrated the stūpa containing the holy relics of Dharma lord Sakya Paṇḍita. Having completed the consecration, Chögyal Phagpa intended to return to Ü-Tsang in central Tibet, take full monastic ordination, and receive further teachings from Uyukpa, according to the advice that had been given him previously by Sakya Paṇḍita. When he arrived in Kham, however, travelers coming from Ü-Tsang told him that Uyukpa had already passed away in the Ox Year. Upon receiving this news, Chögyal Phagpa returned to China, and he arrived at the same moment that the emperor was returning to his palace from Jang. Thus the two were reunited.

On the fifteenth day of the fifth month of the Female Wood Rabbit Year (1255), Chögyal Phagpa took full monastic ordination from the Nyethang abbot, Drakpa Sengé, on the banks of a large river at Thelé, on the Chinese-Mongolian border. Chögyal Phagpa invited Drakpa Sengé to come from Tibet with the following letter:

> *Om syasti siddham*
> Prostrations to the guru and Mañjuśri. Prostrations to the feet of the lord of Dharma, who is the embodiment of the nondual wisdom of all the tathāgatas of the three times and of all the glorious teachers. I write this petition with pure and genuine motivation. You, great master, were born in an immaculate body possessing the seven unique qualities of higher birth, which are the products of the excellent accumulations of merit and wisdom. As a result of previous aspirations, you are a captain of diligence sailing the boat of inexhaustible intelligence in the oceans of learned lamas who are well accomplished in the

three precepts and who capture precious jewels in their nets of detailed analysis. Adorned with these precious qualities, you are outstanding among many learned ones.

Great being who fulfills the wishes of countless others, teacher of gods and humans, O Master Drakpa Sengé, I, the Vajradhara novice monk known as Lodrö Gyaltsen Palsangpo, supplicate you with devotion, and I humbly present this petition without pride or conceit. As you know, my lama, the lord of Dharma who possessed infinite, objectless compassion and flawless wisdom and who performed vast deeds for other beings' benefit throughout the three realms of existence, proclaimed that he would achieve perfect enlightenment as Tathāgata Vimala śrī and would emanate in countless forms. He has now entered *mahāparinirvāṇa*.

However, before doing so, my lord lama told his disciples, "You will be considered excellent in every aspect, the emperor will reign well, and the nation will be at peace. Everyone in Tibet, including the Bönpo, are free at this time from military conscription and taxation. Because the emperor and I have the teacher-disciple relationship, he has granted Tibetans special dispensations and they live in peace. Further, the emperor has decreed that all followers of Buddhism should be led by the Sakyapa.

I am sending a messenger with offerings and this letter of invitation. While the lord of Dharma, Sakya Paṇḍita, was alive, we agreed that, due to my activities and the constraints of time, I would be unable to complete my Dharma education right away. Nevertheless, we both wanted you to come and give Dharma teachings. I asked the guru if it would be suitable to receive full ordination as abbot or master. He said that it would be, and he sent you a letter of invitation. I have also repeatedly sent letters of request. Had you been able to come while Sakya Paṇḍita was still among us, he would have been most pleased. Even had he passed away while you were here, he would have been happy for you to carry on his holy activities. However, you did not come during his lifetime. I do not know the reason, but I am disappointed.

Still, since my Dharma lord has passed away, I have no desire for any teacher other than you. I would like to receive many Dharma teachings from you, including the vinaya, *prajñāpāramitā,* and *pramāṇa.* Just before Sakya Paṇḍita entered into nirvāṇa, he told me, "I have one concern, which is that you have been unable to receive the vows of full ordination. Apart from that, I have no worries." Those of us who were his close disciples supplicated him, "Please do not leave us, but remain and live long." He said, "That would be very difficult." I asked him, "If you cannot remain to become my abbot, then whom should I request?" He replied, "In our times, Master Drakpa Sengé is the most learned teacher and holds the purest discipline. In the three provinces of Tibet, including Kham, there is none more accomplished than he. He is the equivalent of the great Indian Master Śāntipa."

In this way Sakya Paṇḍita indicated that I should petition you, and I do so in fulfillment of his wishes. If you cannot be my abbot, I see no possibility of taking full ordination in this lifetime, knowing no one else suitable for this role. Also, I would miss many Dharma teachings that I intend to request from you. The situation is in your hands. Since my lord of Dharma no longer dwells on this earth, know that you are my only hope. If you could come, I would accept you as my Dharma teacher undifferentiated from the lord of Dharma, Sakya Paṇḍita. Please honor this samaya bond.

If anything in this petition is untrue, or if there has been a distortion of my intention, the vajra of primordial wisdom of the great Vajradhara will crush my heart into a hundred pieces. May the holy beings who possess the eye of wisdom, as well as the guru and the buddhas, witness these words.

I also offer the essence of this petition in verse:

My guru has entered into nirvāṇa,

The maṇḍala of his emanation has vanished into space,
The sun of wisdom has set,
The many clouds of compassion have evaporated,
The continuation of the rain of samaya has been broken,
Alas, because I have seen these ordinary perceptions.
Consequently, I supplicate you again and again,
If you do not gaze upon me with compassion,
Who will show me the path?
When writing this petition, I remember the qualities of the guru.
You live at a vast distance.
Recalling these obstacles,
I shed tears.
Through the power of my teacher's kindness,
And through your compassion,
May this heartfelt request be fulfilled
Just as I wish.
If you do not heed this supplication,
Where is your sense of responsibility and honor?
Where is the samaya, and what has become of compassion?
If one being supplicates another with tears and cries of despair,
Even though there may be no previous connection between the two,
One will come to the aid of the other.
Therefore why not act with compassion in this situation?
By merely glancing at this petition,
Your holy body will be urged to action
Like a horse whipped by the crop of compassion.
Through the perfection of diligence,
May you journey here swiftly.

I should come to you, prostrate before you, and take full ordination in Sakya. This is my wish, but because of circumstances and conditions, we must meet here. As to your travel, it will be easy for you because peace prevails and everyone accords me respect. Know that all the inhabitants of the eastern province are my disciples. I have advised Khamchuwa about the contents of this message. He is prepared to provide any service you require. As a token of good faith, and to provide for your journey, our emperor is sending you fifty large measures of silver coins. In the future, when you are here, teacher and disciples will rejoice in the Dharma and in auspicious material offerings gained through right livelihood.

This petition was written on the third day of the middle month of the Male Water Rabbit Year in the shrine room of the Lingchu tserkhap Palace. May auspiciousness prevail!

Thus did Chögyal Phagpa invite Drakpa Sengé, and upon receiving the letter Drakpa Sengé agreed to come and made the journey. Then it came to pass that before long, Chögyal Phagpa received full ordination. Drakpa Sengé took the role of abbot. Joden Jangpa Sönam Gyaltsen served as master, and Yarlungpa Jangchup Gyaltsen served as *sangtönpa* (secret master). In addition, Chöjé Ürgyen, the abbot of Darapa, Nampharwa Tsulrin, and twenty other fully ordained monks completed the assembly.

Chögyal Phagpa then received prajñāpāramitā teachings from Drakpa Sengé, teachings on vinaya and prātimokṣa from Master Sönam Gyaltsen, and many teachings on logic, such as the seven treatises on pramāṇa, from Yarlungpa Jangchup Gyaltsen. After this, he embarked on a program of detailed personal study.

On the twenty-third of the month, the emperor arranged for the assembly to make a pilgrimage to the sacred Five Peak Mountain. Later, Chögyal Phagpa received many other teachings and empowerments, including the four symbols of Yamāntaka; Mahāmāyā; Vajradhātu; commentaries on the Kālacakra Tantra, including the supplementary commentaries; the collection of reasoning; the collection of homages by Nāgārjuna; and teachings on the Abhidharma.

That same year, on the evening of the thirteenth day of the fourth month, Chögyal Phagpa had a clear vision of Sakya Paṇḍita, who prophesied, "In one hundred thousand years you will achieve the excellent *siddhi* of *mahāmudrā*." Upon hearing this, Chögyal Phagpa felt as though new life had been breathed into him. He paid homage to his teacher, saying:

> I, who have long experienced the anguish
> Of the many sufferings of existence,
> Have now been given the breath of life through your
> holy words.
> I prostrate and pay homage to you, lord of Dharma,
> Treasure of compassion and master of wisdom.

With this homage, he wrote the verses of the inner offering known as Thöpa Gyatso.

Later, Chögyal Phagpa created a written script for the benefit of the Mongolian people, who had previously had none. As a sign of his appreciation, the emperor gave Chögyal Phagpa the Strengthening Buddhism decree, and the text of this decree was woven into silk brocade.

Chögyal Phagpa then turned the wheel of Dharma in the emperor's palace. Many learned Hashang Chinese masters who were followers of the teacher Sinshing attended these Dharma gatherings. They were strongly attached to their tradition and view, and the emperor, foreseeing that they would distort the pure Buddhist teachings, asked Chögyal Phagpa to enter into debate with them and defeat them. He then selected seventeen of the most learned masters of that tradition and set a date for the contest. Chögyal Phagpa defeated them all, placed them in the right view, and established them on the Buddhist path as ordained monks.

At the age of twenty-eight, Chögyal Phagpa sent many valuable things to the Sakya Monastery and advised the leader of the Sakya region, Śākyaśrībhadra, to complete the monastery's construction. In response, Śākyaśrībhadra built a shrine called Serthok Chenmo, or "Golden Pagoda," to the west of the shrine known as Ütsé Nyingma.

In the Female Wood Ox Year (1265), Chögyal Phagpa, age thirty-one, returned to Sakya. There he built a stūpa known as Tashi Gomang ("Many Auspicious Doors"), encrusted with precious gems and containing the deities of Vajradhātu. This stūpa was placed inside the Golden Pagoda shrine. In addition, he restored the stūpas of the earlier founders of the Sakya order and had canopies placed atop each of them with a golden roof above. He also had constructed an immense Dharma wheel of copper plated with gold. Inside the monastery, Chögyal Phagpa sponsored the writing in pure gold ink of over two hundred volumes of the Buddha's teachings, including sūtras, tantras, and prajñāpāramitā. He turned the wheel of Dharma on many occasions before large assemblies, bringing them to spiritual maturity and liberation.

Although Chögyal Phagpa had completed his education and was a lord of Dharma, he remained without conceit, and, in order to strengthen his devotion to the Dharma, he continued to rely upon spiritual teachers. Among them were the great Kashmiri Paṇḍita Śrī Tathāgatabhadra (in Sanskrit, Śākyaśrībhandra), the translator from Mustang, Lowo Lotsawa Sherab Rinchen, Narthang Abbot Chim Namkhadrak, Sangwanyen Ösung Gönpo, the great Mahāsiddha Yöntenpal, Gyerbuba Tsokgom Kungapal, Shangshungpa Dorjé Óser, Rinpoche Kyopapal, Rangwen Marpa Nalior Wangchuk Galo, Chak Lotsawa's master Nyima Pal, Epashang Ngönpawa Rinpoché Dorjé; Drakphukpa Gewai Shenyen Bumpa Öser, Doklowa Dulzin Shākya Jangchup, Rongpa Khenpo Sengé Silnön, master in Abhidharma Ngönpawa Wangchuk Tsondrü, master of Rong Rilung Phukpa, Chökyi Gönpo, Jilbubai Geshé Taktön Sherab Óser, Üdepa Lopön Sangyé Bum, Geshé Drekhüpa, Lhajé Darma Sengé, and many other others.

From some of these Chögyal Phagpa learned Śrāvakayāna teachings; from others, Mahāyāna teachings; and from yet others, Vajrayāna. In short, he studied nearly all the Dharma that was extant in Tibet at that time, including the five major Buddhist sciences, the Tripiṭaka, the four classes of tantra, and all the treatises related to sūtras and tantras. He also received empowerments, blessings, instructions, and pith instructions with their supplements. In this way, he worked with great diligence and dedicated all that he had toward the growth of the Buddhist doctrine and the benefit of all sentient beings.

In the Female Fire Rabbit Year (1268), at age thirty-three, Chögyal Phagpa again received an invitation from Kublai Khan to return to China. Preparing for the journey, he assembled thirteen categories of retainers to accompany him. At this time, a Tibetan master known as Chomden Raldri sent him a critical letter, which said:

> The Buddhist doctrines of the Kadampa and Chagyapa have been obscured by clouds;
> The welfare and happiness of beings are controlled by foreigners;
> A degenerate monk appears as a secular leader.
> Since you do not recognize these three facts, I know you are not a holy being.

Chögyal Phagpa replied:

> The waxing and waning of the doctrine was taught by Buddha;
> The welfare and happiness of beings depend upon their individual karma;
> Forms appear suitable to beings' needs.
> Since you do not realize these three facts, I know you are not learned.

The *Dungrab Yarap Khagyen* states that the thirteen categories of attendants that Chögyal Phagpa assembled consisted of the following: both outer and inner attendants, chamber staff, food servers, shrine masters, appointment keepers, secretaries, treasurers, cooks, household staff, throne managers, grooms, animal keepers, special assistants, and keepers of small pets. Although there are different ways of categorizing the retainers, this is the list recorded in that reliable source.

Master Chögyal Phagpa was invited to China by the emperor, and seeing that countless disciples could be tamed by his Dharma teaching, Chögyal Phagpa compassionately agreed to go. During this journey, Namkhabum met him and spent considerable time with him discussing the holy Dharma. Namkhabum saw Chögyal Phagpa as a great and advanced bodhisattva, and, as a result, Namkhabum developed unshakable devotion toward Chögyal Phagpa. Having received vast and profound Dharma teachings, including the bodhisattva vow and other things, he wrote down many quotations from Chögyal Phagpa's holy teachings that demonstrate the master's truly extraordinary qualities.

On the way to China, Chögyal Phagpa gave countless empowerments and instructions to many fortunate disciples, placing them in a state of maturity and liberation. When he reached China, he was like the sun surrounded by brilliant rays of light or like the moon surrounded by countless stars. It could also be said that he was like a buddha surrounded by countless *śrāvakas*, disciples, and saṅgha members. From a mundane point of view, he was surrounded by a large assembly of learned disciples and other attendants who, with him, had endured many hardships on the way to China, crossing narrow mountain passes and large rivers. To be unconcerned by such hardships is one of the hallmarks of a bodhisattva. In the sūtras the Lord Buddha states, "Bodhisattvas would travel even hundreds of *yojanas* to give Dharma teachings to sentient beings, without considering the hardship to themselves."

When Chögyal Phagpa arrived in China, the emperor's eldest son, his wife, and many ministers were present together with a large gathering. The lama arrived seated upon an Indian elephant adorned with jewels. To his right and left were many victory banners, countless musicians playing instruments, and lavish offerings. Chögyal Phagpa gave countless vast and profound Dharma teachings through which the doctrine of Buddhism arose in China like the sun in the morning sky.

The following year, the leader of the Sakya region, Śākyaśrībhadra, laid the foundation of the Lhakang Chenmo. He and another leader, Kunga Sangpo, were able to encourage the thirteen groups of ten thousand families to help with the construction. In addition, they built the Rinchen Gang Labrang, the Lhakang Labrang, and the Duchö Labrang.

Some time later, in the Male Iron Horse Year (1271), the emperor of China requested that Chögyal Phagpa, then age thirty-six, bestow empowerments upon him. After receiving the empowerments, he offered Chögyal Phagpa a six-pointed crystal seal known as the Sheldam Lingdrukma, similar to that owned by the king of Minyak. He also bestowed upon Chögyal Phagpa a decree of special recognition, saying, "You are the only son of the gods on earth and under heaven, an emanation of the Buddha, creator of the nation's script, national peacemaker, great paṇḍita who is most learned in the five types of knowledge, teacher of the emperor, Chögyal Phagpa Tishri." With this decree, he made immense offerings of precious things, including one thousand large measures of silver and fifty-nine thousand bolts of silk and other fabrics. Whenever the emperor encountered Chögyal Phagpa, he offered him a special *khata* and a large measure of silver.

The emperor's combined offerings during Chögyal Phagpa's first and second visits to China amounted to one hundred measures of gold, over one thousand measures of silver, over fifty thousand bolts of silk, and many other items. In turn, Chögyal Phagpa placed the whole of the Mongolian population on the Mahāyāna path and spread the Buddha's doctrine like the sun throughout all of China.

Chögyal Phagpa prepared to return to Tibet, telling the emperor that he would come back to China soon. However, as Chögyal Phagpa was preparing to depart, the emperor had a vision that his teacher would not remain for long in this world. As a result, both the teacher and the emperor suffered greatly at their pending separation. For this reason, Chögyal Phagpa's progress in leaving China was slow, extending to weeks, months, and years.

Arriving in the foothills of Mount Pomralha near the Machu River, the emperor and Chögyal Phagpa took their final leave of one another. Just before parting, they were together for a time like the sun and the moon, surrounded by the emperor's retinue of four army divisions and more than one hundred thousand followers. The emperor made immeasurable offerings, gave a splendid farewell reception, and accorded Chögyal Phagpa the highest possible veneration.

At that time, many auspicious signs appeared on the earth and in the sky. A white cloud shaped like an elephant's trunk extended toward the earth from the southeast. Upon this cloud appeared clearly the mahāsiddha Virūpa, the master Sachen Kunga Nyingpo, and many other Indian and Tibetan lineage lamas, surrounded by buddhas and bodhisattvas. These were clearly perceived even by ordinary beings. It is also said that many auspicious signs of bodhisattvas appeared, performing benefit for beings in other realms of existence.

Through the blessings of the holy body, voice, and mind of Master Chögyal Phagpa, whose birth name was Lodrö Gyaltsen Palsangpo, the subjects of the Mongolian emperor had the seeds of white deeds planted in their minds. They attained higher rebirth through pure aspirations, and they trusted strongly in the Dharma in the three ways. Through this, they were placed on the path of liberation and guided toward the unsurpassable state.

Having accomplished these great deeds for the benefit of China and Mongolia, this compassionate great master returned to the Land of Snows for the benefit of beings there. Where the terrain was impassable, roads and bridges were built with the cooperation of humans and nonhumans alike. He arrived in Sakya, his main seat, with a large retinue. There, many humans and nonhumans welcomed him with offerings and other signs of veneration.

For his part, Chögyal Phagpa gave Dharma teachings and material wealth everywhere he went. Anyone who saw or heard of his holy activities was amazed; the hairs of their bodies stood on end, and tears came to their eyes. In brief, Chögyal Phagpa gave Dharma teachings according to the varied capacities and needs of beings, and placed them on the path of maturation and liberation.

In the Year of the Rabbit (1276), at age forty-one, Chögyal Phagpa arrived at the Sakya Monastery. Many learned masters of Ü-Tsang joined him, together with the leaders of nearby regions who wished to receive teaching and advice. Because Chögyal Phagpa's renown spread as far as India, Kashmir, and other countries, paṇḍitas from these places began arriving in Sakya to receive his teachings. Each of them venerated him, made offerings according to their ability, and requested teachings according to their needs. Chögyal Phagpa himself said, "I have received almost all of the teachings concerning the sūtras and tantras, including the pith instructions, and even the most minor teachings. I have, in fact, received nearly every teaching that has come to Tibet from India. I possess the authentic source, and you may therefore request any teaching you like from me according to your wish." So saying, he gave countless vast and profound Dharma teachings according to beings' needs, withholding nothing. He also helped many sentient beings with vast material gifts. In this way he worked day and night at the Sakya Monastery to benefit all beings.

In mid-spring of the Female Fire Ox Year (1277), the lord of Dharma, Chögyal Phagpa, turned the wheel of Dharma at Tsang Chumik Ringmo. A son of the emperor sponsored this teaching, during which Chögyal Phagpa honored more than seventy thousand monks by giving each one generous food offerings, a gold coin, and one bolt of woolen cloth for their Dharma robes. Many thousands of highly learned Dharma masters were also present. Counting ordinary beings alone, the crowd exceeded one hundred thousand people.

Chögyal Phagpa turned the vast and profound wheel of Dharma extensively, giving the Mahāyāna bodhisattva vow, which is the unique path for all buddhas of the past, present, and future, planting in the minds of everyone present the seeds for reaching unsurpassable enlightenment. He also wrote a Dharma text known as *Description of Teachers and Their Doctrine*. In this work he wrote, "I, the fully ordained monk and vajra holder Chögyal Phagpa, performed the bodhisattva's vow for a gathering of over one hundred thousand persons. On that auspicious day I also wrote this text." So it came to pass that this great master turned the wheel of Dharma for more than fourteen days.

A soft rain fell one morning, a few days after the teachings began. A great wind then arose that completely blew away all of the dust and dirt. This was followed by a shower of flowers mixed with snow and sleet that cleansed the ground and left it strewn with flowers. Everyone present became aware of a pervasive scent of perfume like they had never smelled before. When the crowd gathered in the morning, they all saw the sun encircled by five layers of rainbows and celestial offerings being made in space. Eleven great masters possessing pure perception and twelve *ching sang* also possessing pure perception saw buddhas and bodhisattvas inside the rainbow circles, all emanating light rays. This miraculous vision filled the whole of space. At the same time, vast material offerings were arranged on the roof of the hall, and a silk carpet was laid out, woven with Chögyal Phagpa's hand, foot, and head prints. Chögyal Phagpa stood on this carpet and, reciting the Petition to the Buddhas of the Ten Directions, made offerings to the buddhas and bodhisattvas as vast as those made by Samantabhadra.

One evening some time later, several of Chögyal Phagpa's chief disciples, including the twelve ching sang, smelled what seemed to be roasting flesh near Chögyal Phagpa's dwelling place. The odor made them sick and some vomited. One of the disciples, Yöntri , inquired about the cause of the smell. Chögyal Phagpa said, "Eighty *vidyādharas* have arrived here in the sky. To welcome them, the *vīras* and *dākinīs* from this area and from other holy places have made offerings. That odor comes from the eight great cemeteries, and it cannot be tolerated by ordinary humans. This is why the ching sang feel ill. I do not fault them."

With this, he took nectar from the skullcup on his table and placed it on the tongue of each of his disciples. Immediately they were restored to health, and their minds became very clear. In front of them appeared the eighty vidyādharas, including Nāgārjuna flanked by the mahāsiddha Virūpa on his right and the mahāsiddha Padmavajra on his left, along with countless other vidyādharas, vīras, and dākinīs completely filling the space. The vidyādharas placed their hands on Chögyal Phagpa's head, gave him Dharma instructions and prophecies, commended him for his holy activities, and recited auspicious verses.

On the fourteenth day, when he had completely accomplished the turning of the wheel of Dharma, Chögyal Phagpa stood before the gathering and gave a detailed explanation of the dedication of merit. Starting early in the morning on that day, auspicious omens pervaded space. General auspicious signs, such as rainbows and showers of flowers, also appeared on each day of the teachings.

At this time, the chief scholar of the Narthang region, Chomden Raldri, felt himself to be superior and he did not bother to attend Chögyal Phagpa's teachings. He did, however, read some of Chögyal Phagpa's biography. On the fourteenth day of Chögyal Phagpa's teachings, he said to himself, "If I do not attend to Chögyal Phagpa's activities, I will be guilty of ignorance. Through his spiritual power he has greatly influenced ordinary beings and learned masters. I must go and see for myself what manner of being he is and what he is doing." With that in mind, he changed clothes and started out for the teaching.

Along the way, on a pass southwest of Narthang, he passed a place with creeks and a cave from which voices emanated. Looking into the cave, he saw sixteen elderly monks wearing tattered Dharma robes. Seeing this he thought, "This great being, Chögyal Phagpa, is unlike other masters. Even these senior monks, near the end of their lives and who surely find it difficult to travel, nonetheless are determined to attend Chögyal Phagpa's teachings."

Reaching Tsang Chumik Ringmo, he found Chögyal Phagpa seated upon the Dharma throne amid an ocean-like assembly of monks and laypeople. His body was adorned with the major and minor marks of perfection, his voice proclaimed the vast and profound Dharma with the combination of unborn sound and emptiness, and his mind rested in the multiple *samādhi* of bliss and emptiness. The moment Chomden Raldri beheld this holy teacher, his mind was completely overwhelmed and he could think of nothing but Chögyal Phagpa's power.

When the teaching ended, Chögyal Phagpa explained the dedication of merit and ascended to the roof of the hall while the rest of the gathering remained in their places. Chomden Raldri himself could smell a delightful scent like nothing he had experienced before. He then went to Chögyal Phagpa's personal quarters, situated below the golden monastery pagoda, and examined the inside and outside of Chögyal Phagpa's shrine hall. Inside, near the top, were sixteen Dharma thrones and upon each of them were stacked five cushions. Extensive material offerings had been placed before them. Immediately, Chomden Raldri recalled the sixteen elderly monks he had seen on his way to the teachings, and he thought, "Until now I have been ruled by my own conceit. In fact, this great master is not an ordinary being." Feeling great regret at not having attended the teachings, he thought, "I should erase all doubt about this great lama from my mind." At that moment, the scent of perfume intensified, and he beheld the sixteen arhats upon the sixteen thrones. Chögyal Phagpa was reciting the Sevenfold Prayer and making offerings to them.

Feeling yet deeper chagrin, Chomden Raldri performed countless prostrations and confessed his fault. From that moment, his mind became completely serene and devoid of pride. Ultimately, he became strongly devoted to Chögyal Phagpa and composed an elegant praise to him known as the *Sound of Brahmā's Thunderbolt.* Later in his life, he was venerated by the Mongolian emperor as a great scholar and received great offerings, which were brought to Narthang by the emperor's messengers.

In this way, Chögyal Phagpa performed miraculous displays of his accomplishment inconceivable to ordinary beings. He sponsored the writing of 115 volumes of scriptures in gold ink, which were placed in the Do Kham Gang (Eastern Tibet) Shrine, and fourteen volumes of sūtras in gold ink in Takthog Shimocher. At the Sakya Monastery, he built a stūpa for Sakya Paṇḍita's holy relics, constructed like Tashi Gomang and made of gold. He placed the stūpa inside a shrine hall and erected a golden pagoda on the top. He performed these and many other holy activities for the benefit of the doctrine. In short, though he daily received limitless material offerings from every direction, he kept nothing for himself, not even a portion of the value of a sesame seed. Everything given him was either offered to the Triple Gem or distributed to the poor.

Chögyal Phagpa became one of the best-endowed teachers in the history of Buddhism. During his lifetime, he was offered six sets of the Kangyur, and he himself sponsored over 2,157 volumes of texts written in gold ink. The Mongolian emperor twice offered him over one thousand large measures of silver, as well as gold and countless other offerings. Chögyal Phagpa dedicated all these for the benefit of the doctrine and sentient beings.

Chögyal Phagpa also benefited beings by preserving pure moral conduct, and serving as abbot for 1,425 ordination ceremonies for monks and nuns. One of his chief disciples, Chökyi Gönpo, served as abbot for 947 full ordination and novice ceremonies in one year alone. Through this master and his disciples and lineage, the ordination of monks and nuns spread throughout China, Mongolia, and Tibet.

Outwardly, through the samādhi precepts, Chögyal Phagpa appeared as a scholar, performing learned activities such as teaching, debating, and composing. Inwardly, his mind never wavered from single-pointed concentration. As a result, he directly perceived a multitude of tutelary deities and experienced unbroken luminosity in his holy mind. These and other qualities are beyond description in ordinary terms.

Chögyal Phagpa possessed other boundless good qualities, such as unimpeded heightened perception. For example, just before seeing the Jowo statue in Kyidrong, he saw Avalokiteśvara in a dream and composed a song of praise to him. Another time, when Sakya Paṇḍita was traveling to Mongolia, a close disciple of Sakya Paṇḍita named Jé Yangönpa approached him, saying, "While you are traveling to China and Mongolia, your disciples require a strong teacher who will act as regent in your place. We will make him an object of devotion. Will your nephew Chögyal Phagpa one day be as qualified as you?" Sakya Paṇḍita replied, "My nephew will be an authentic teacher." At that moment, Chögyal Phagpa was resting a ways off, napping without closing his eyes. Pointing to that, Sakya Paṇḍita said, "That is a sign of one who can recognize the clear light. In general, the pure lineage of my ancestors is such that they can recognize some amount of unbroken clear light."

Another time, an Indian master known as Paṇḍita Gotamabhadra had a remarkable dream. The next morning, Chögyal Phagpa, through his powers of heightened perception, recounted the dream in full detail. Paṇḍita Gotamabhadra was amazed, and he thought, "This guru has great powers of clairvoyance." He then developed great devotion to Chögyal Phagpa.

Once, when Chögyal Phagpa was dwelling at Uyuk, several tax collectors were also traveling in the area. Meanwhile, a man known as Joden from Shang Lhabu arrived to visit Chögyal Phagpa. When he arrived, the first thing he saw was a group of Mongolians surrounding Chögyal Phagpa's dwelling and killing many of the local animals. Inside Chögyal Phagpa's yurt he saw a secretary on the right composing Dharma scriptures, another on the left answering correspondence, and before him a monk making *tormas*. Chögyal Phagpa himself was making torma offerings.

Joden thought, "What kind of a lama is this? He surrounds himself with Mongolian barbarians who harm animals, while one of his secretaries appears to be writing letters of refusal to the petitions of beings. What is the use of his having a secretary composing Dharma scriptures if it doesn't benefit his own mind? Further, he is making torma offerings without uttering a single word of dedication. This is unacceptable. He is not an authentic religious teacher."

The moment these thoughts crossed Joden's mind, Chögyal Phagpa looked at him and said, "Regarding the torma, if merit is to be had from preparing the offering, it will be received by the monk doing the preparation. If merit is to be had from meditation, it will be received by myself, who is doing the meditating. And if it is to be had from dedication, then you do the dedicating."

Realizing immediately that Chögyal Phagpa had unimpeded higher perception, Joden was afraid and regretted his impure perception. He confessed his error and made many prostrations. Being truly amazed at Chögyal Phagpa's ability, he told everyone he saw about this incident. He realized that Chögyal Phagpa's holy activity was performed according to the needs of beings, and that the animal slaughter and tax collection pertained to the karma of the individuals rather than to Chögyal Phagpa.

Through these and many other stories, Chögyal Phagpa's powers of clairvoyance were widely broadcast. Because he was such a holy person who possessed unimpeded clairvoyance and a multitude of good qualities, he was able to perform vast activities for the Buddha's doctrine without hindrance. Through his writing, teaching, and countless other activities, Chögyal Phagpa approximated the accomplishments of Indian teachers of the past such as Nāgārjuna.

His compositions were easy to understand and elegant in style, and their meaning was profound and in accordance with the sūtras and tantras. He produced a multitude of root texts, commentaries on sūtras and tantras, letters responding to questions, advice for countless beings, and praises and supplication prayers to lamas and deities. Whatever Chögyal Phagpa wrote was pleasing to hear, easy to understand, meaningful, and readily recollected by those who heard it. His writings have remained popular to this day. Chögyal Phagpa thus spread the precious doctrine of the *sugata* in every direction like the rays of the sun.

Through teaching, composing, and debating Chögyal Phagpa produced innumerable disciples in China and Tibet. Among them, the chief disciples holding the lineage of explanation were great masters from the three directions known as East, West, and Center. These and many other teachers, including Lama Drakpa Öser, Lama Tashi Pal, Malo, and others, held his teaching lineage. Among the disciples holding his meditation lineage there were many who received empowerments and pith instructions, integrating their practice with their life.

Among those who received the complete pith instructions in the same manner in which the contents of one vase are poured into another were the masters Shang Könchok Pal and Gelong Kunlo. Others upholding his teaching lineage were Laruwa, Nyenchenpa, Sulungpa, Oserbum from Salwa, Üdepa Lopön Sangyé Bum, and other great masters. In short, during his lifetime and that of his chief disciple, the Buddha's doctrine spread in a way that can be compared to its dissemination in India at the time of the Buddha himself.

Through his clairvoyance, Chögyal Phagpa placed countless beings on the stage of maturation and liberation, each according to their ability. But the time came when he perceived that in future lives he would perform vast benefit for sentient beings and that it was time to leave this life. Calling Dharmapāla Rakṣita to his side, he said, "Through the holy biographies of the great Sakyapa lamas we know that they performed great benefit for the Buddha's doctrine and sentient beings. For myself, I have acted according to my ability to benefit beings as widely as possible. Now is the time for you to take this responsibility, so be alerted."

In his youth, Chögyal Phagpa had a dream one night in which he was holding a bamboo cane with eighty knots, and the forty-sixth knot was crooked. When he related the dream to Sakya Paṇḍita, the latter explained that it represented his life span. The forty-sixth knot indicated that obstacles would arise when he reached that age and that he should take precautions at that time. In this way, Sakya Paṇḍita prophesied the span of Chögyal Phagpa's life. Sakya Paṇḍita also prophesied that when Chögyal Phagpa approached the time of entering into parinirvāṇa, many celestial beings with clairvoyant minds, delighting in the Buddha's doctrine, would know that this great being would no longer remain on earth and would think, "If he departs to other realms, who will uphold the Buddha's precious doctrine?" They would then enter into a state of mourning and despair. Not only did this come to pass as prophesied, but many birds chirped discordantly as well and their feathers faded. Even the sun was not as bright, and the constellations of stars failed to move according to the celestial order. Ordinary humans felt unrest and indecision, and meditators in caves found themselves unable to concentrate single-pointedly. Students and teachers took less pleasure in hearing and teaching the Dharma, and they became inclined to distraction. Because land-owning spirits were unhappy, the crops that year were poor. Just as shadows fall in the valley when the sun sets in the west, these signs indicated the degeneration of spirit that occurs when great beings depart for other realms because the happiness of ordinary beings depends upon holy teachers such as Chögyal Phagpa. And at this time, Chögyal Phagpa himself saw in his pure vision that he was being venerated and given offerings like those of Samantabhadra by countless bodhisattvas in Sukhāvatī, the realm of the red Buddha Amitābha, and in many other buddha fields.

On the night of the third day of the tenth month in the Year of the Dragon (1280), Chögyal Phagpa dreamed that he reached Glorious Southern Mountain in India where Master Nāgārjuna was seated in front of an enormous bodhi tree. He was listening to the six collections of Madhyamaka teachings and many other Dharmas. At the same time, from the sky many goddesses, most notably Knowledge Queen Majachenmo, clearly appeared in space and made countless offerings. These and many other auspicious signs appeared to him both day and night.

Chögyal Phagpa began the annual anniversary offering to Sakya Paṇḍita on the first day of the tenth month, and he continued to make great offerings throughout that month. His attendants said to him, "Sakya Paṇḍita's annual offering is in the eleventh month, not the tenth. Why are you doing this early?" He replied, "We usually begin in the eleventh month. However, I made a commitment to do it for an entire month every year, and I fear that I might be unable to complete my commitment this year if I wait until next month to start making maṇḍala offerings. Thus I have begun a month early." He continued performing the offerings until the eighteenth day of the eleventh month, presiding over the ceremonies each day.

On the nineteenth, twentieth, and twenty-first days he remained in his room. Early in the morning on the twenty-second day, he asked his attendants to arrange an elaborate offering. When they had done so, he took his vajra and bell in hand and manifested entering into parinirvāṇa amid many auspicious signs such as a rain of flowers, a display of light rays, and the sound of celestial music. Chögyal Phagpa entered mahāparinirvāṇa at the age of forty-six in the Male Iron Dragon Year (1280) in order to dispel the wrong views of those who cling to entities as permanent, to demonstrate diligence for those who are lazy, and to benefit beings in other realms. At that time, the earth trembled in six different ways in the Sakya region and a delicious fragrance, never smelled before, pervaded space. Many other celestial offerings appeared.

During his lifetime, Chögyal Phagpa engaged in many activities. He taught the Dharma, built great monasteries, accepted spiritual and political responsibility for the Tibetan people, and traveled between China and Tibet. He worked diligently for the benefit of the Buddha's doctrine and for sentient beings. However, some unfortunate beings who lacked good karma held disrespectful views toward his holy activities. Because these individuals broke their samaya, many of Chögyal Phagpa's bones turned dark when his holy body was cremated.

During the cremation ceremony, one of Chögyal Phagpa's chief disciples, Drakpa Shönu, said to be an emanation of Blue Mañjuśrī, approached the site and strongly supplicated the guru with loud lamentations, beating his head against the stūpa. While this was happening, a piece of charcoal flew out of the stūpa. Within it, Drakpa Shönu discovered a relic of Chögyal Phagpa's thumb, its surface bearing clear outlines of the five dhyani buddhas, traced as finely as if they were executed by an artist.

Again, Drakpa Shönu supplicated the guru, placing the relic on his own head. After this, the designs on the relic became yet clearer, so that even the faces and the hands of the buddhas could be discerned. Later, he placed the relic inside an image of the Buddha and kept it in a shrine in Shangdud Monastery. This is known as the "Special Shrine of Master Drakpa Shönu." Later, it was recorded that the relic was removed from the statue and kept by the Gyatso family. The relic and the statue both came into the possession of Lhasa Zongpa, after which it was offered to Jetsun Dampa Kunga Drolchok. From him it came to me, Sakyapa Ngawang Kunga Sönam.

The dark relics, and even the news of Chögyal Phagpa's death itself, were kept secret lest trouble be made by the emperor. No one dared travel to China to tell him. Finally, the dark relics were mixed with pieces of ivory, and the shrine master, Drakpa Öser, offered to go to China to inform the emperor of events. "Even if I am punished," thought Drakpa Öser, "I will have no regret. I am doing this for my teacher and out of respect for the karmic links between him and the emperor." So saying, he took the relics and left for China.

As he neared the emperor's palace, he followed the same daily meditation routine that Chögyal Phagpa himself followed. When the emperor heard that a master nearby was performing the same daily meditations as Chögyal Phagpa, he sent a party to inquire who the master might be. When they arrived, they recognized him as Chögyal Phagpa's shrine master. Learning of this, the emperor invited Drakpa Öser to his palace. The latter refrained for a time from speaking of Chögyal Phagpa's death, instead giving many Dharma teachings, and the emperor was delighted with Drakpa Öser's skill.

After they had established the teacher-disciple relationship, Drakpa Öser gave the emperor the news of Chögyal Phagpa's death. He also offered the emperor Chögyal Phagpa's relics, placing them on the emperor's head and instructing him to make prayers and supplications.

After the emperor had done this, he opened the relic box and found that the contents had turned into pearl-like *ringsel*. "These are my teacher's relics," the emperor said. He tossed aside the ivory that had been mixed with the bones, saying, "These are not true relics." He then sent some of the ringsel back to Tibet for the benefit of disciples there.

In ancient times you were the emanation Lotsawa Paltsek.
Later, you appeared as the bodhisattva Satön Ri.
In this life, you appeared in the northern region, in the Land of
  Snows,
Bearing the name of Drogön Chögyal Phagpa.
Soon after you took birth,
There appeared amazing indications of a great being.
The name of the holy being Chögyal Phagpa spread.

You are a Dharma treasure for both scholars and siddhas.
You became lord of all beings in the northern region.
In order to benefit countless beings,
You purposely took birth in the Sakya clan and Khon family,
Became an object of veneration for all,
And demonstrated the meaning of the name "Holy One."
Great rescuer of beings:
Is there anyone who even comes close to you?
Some masters, though rich in Dharma,
Barely have enough material wealth to survive.
Others are materially wealthy, like rulers of nations,
Yet their glorious Dharma is as rare as the appearance of a star in the day.
But you fully unite both of these in one life.
This is a truly amazing sign of achievement.
Your wealth is like that of a universal emperor,
And your glorious Dharma is like that of the lord of the Sakya clan.
No one like you has appeared before,
Nor will anyone like you appear for long.
For this reason, I offer devotion and respect from the depth of my heart.
Through your great kindness,
The name of the Sakyapa and its holy activities
Pervade the land.
Who remains in Ü-Tsang and Kham
Who is not your subject and disciple?

Part Two

A Gift of Dharma to Kublai Khan

2. Root Verses of *A Gift of Dharma to Kublai Khan*

DROGÖN CHÖGYAL PHAGPA

TO THE INCOMPARABLE enlightened one, who is endowed with the splendor of fame in name and the splendor of wondrous virtues (*yönten*) in actual fact, I offer homage.

Although you, noble emperor, already know the discourses on worldly and spiritual science, still, as with the songs and music of musicians to which you listen again and again even when you have heard them all before, why shouldn't a poet repeat wise words?

All the countless teachings of Dharma taught by the sage for the sake of countless disciples indeed are meant to be practiced. But how may this be done?

A subject, bound by fear and a sense of shame, does not disobey his king's command but dwells in right conduct without harming others and, as a result, grows in good fortune and even earns the praises of the king. It is similar with a person who accepts, in accordance with his ability to accomplish them, the rules of discipline enjoined by the sage to help beginners on the Śrāvakayāna and Mahāyāna paths.

If after properly receiving vows from an abbot, that person guards them from a fear of seen and unseen sufferings in worldly existence and from a sense of shame when he reflects, "The multitudes of noble ones who know the thoughts of other beings will be shamed if I break my vows," then, as a result, he will become a foundation not only of seen and unseen joys in worldly existence but also of the virtues of perfect liberation. He will also become a worthy object of veneration for men and gods and even receive the praises of buddhas.

These three realms of existence, after all, are just suffering, while nirvāṇa, too, is just peace. Looking with pity, therefore, on those who wish either for worldly existence or nirvāṇa, the Buddha alone, himself free from sorrow, removes sorrow, and, having himself attained great joy, bestows joy. And he has appeared from among beings like us.

We can use the methods he used. Without timidity and laziness, therefore, you should unwaveringly aspire to win highest enlightenment and feel free to think, "I must surely attain buddhahood."

Guard as your own life the vows you have made that, if violated, will cause you to be burned in hells, and that, if preserved, will enable you to experience truly wonderful results in proceeding from joy to joy even now.

Since the three sets of vows—of the Śrāvakayāna, Mahāyāna, and Vajrayāna paths—are the foundation whereon all virtues may arise, remain, and grow within oneself and others, try from the very first to be firm in their observance.

Become certain that the teaching, which is virtuous in its beginning, middle, and end, and whose words are quite flawless and not contradictory to the two logical proofs of valid knowledge, is the unique spiritual way among ways.

Know, too, that the enlightened one who taught it is endowed with unhindered wisdom and great compassion since he revealed the truth without close-fistedness and with tremendous power.

Because they are his followers and a gathering of beings with virtues similar to his, and because your own sphere of spiritual activity is identical to theirs, know the noble assembly of bodhisattvas to be the best field for increasing your merit.

Realizing that it is your preceptor who points out and introduces you to these Three Jewels, that he is endowed with the same virtues they have, and that he sustains you with kindness, always attend and meditate upon him with unflagging faith.

Since they are like yourself in having the nature of being endowed with the causes of pain and a constant state of unsatisfactoriness, and like yourself in wishing themselves to be free from unhappiness and its causes, you should unceasingly meditate great compassion for all living beings.

Recalling the benefits of virtue that you will need to attain highest enlightenment and to achieve others' good as well as your own purposes, strive wholeheartedly with genuine devotion to acquire it. In brief, since a mind endowed with faith, compassion, and intention is the precursor of all spiritual accomplishments, perform even the smallest virtue with these three present.

Envision the body of the enlightened one either in front of you or as your own body, and visualize that your dwelling place is a buddha field wherein all beings are conquerors surrounded by bodhisattvas and disciples. Then worship yourself and others with oceans of offerings consisting of the enjoyment of the five sense objects.

Realize that your own virtuous preceptor and all the conquerors are truly equal and nondual in form, activity, and essential nature. At all times, you should envision him in front of you, or seated atop the crown of your head or within the lotus of your heart, and pray to him or meditate upon him as nondual with yourself.

Of virtue, nonvirtue, pleasure, pain, and all the phenomena of saṃsāra and nirvāṇa, mind is the substratum.

If you were to examine that mind thoroughly from every angle, you would realize that it has neither color nor shape, nor is it single or manifold. It therefore has no nature; therefore it is not arisen, neither does it remain nor cease. It is devoid of both center and periphery and is thus away from all extremes. It has just the nature of space.

Even so, cognition is not stopped. Hence mind has the nature of nondual cognition and emptiness.

As one's own mind is, so too is the nature of all beings' minds.

Understand thoroughly that all phenomena are nondual appearance and emptiness, and place your mind in meditation without grasping.

Through meditating nondually on the two objects [one's preceptor and the enlightened one] and objectlessness [emptiness], you will attain a superior meditative state of tranquil concentration [*śamatha*] that cannot be disturbed by thoughts.

Joyfully remembering that every act of virtue or nonvirtue increases the strength of one's virtuous or nonvirtuous inclinations, always bring virtues to mind and strengthen them.

You should especially recollect and analyze the support, form, and experience of your meditation whenever you have meditated upon an object. Examining further the interdependent origination of their causes and conditions, however many they may be, you will attain meditative insight [*vidarśanā*] through realizing the true state of their suchness—that is, through realizing that no support, form, or experience whatsoever exists.

Following the performance of virtues, you should gather together all the merits acquired through that [meditation and the like] and fully dedicate them to the attainment of perfect enlightenment by yourself and all these countless beings.

Even though transferable merit may not have been acquired at the time you offer prayers, your wishes nonetheless will be fulfilled if you pray for a great purpose to be achieved, for mind alone is chief.

Every virtue that is adorned by this kind of recollection, dedication, and noble prayer will increase unceasingly and eventually become the cause of great good for oneself and others.

Everything that is experienced and all other conditioned things [*saṃskṛtadharma*]—the five aggregates, senses, sense objects, and sense consciousnesses—are devoid of any nature of their own because they all depend upon causes and conditions.

Therefore you should know that these external objects, appearing in various forms to, and experienced by, mind, which is stained by mental impressions, are not real. They are like magic shows that appear due to a variety of causes. They are also like dreams that occur during sleep.

The so-called unconditioned *dharmas* [*asaṃskṛtadharma*] are simply ascriptions. A person would have to be mad to wish to propose meaningless names for them, or to indulge in thoughts about them and thereby accept them as conditioned dharmas.

Never scorn the connection between deeds and their results, for the teachings on the interdependent origination of cause and result as it operates in the sphere of relative truth are not deceptive. You will experience the ripening results of your actions.

There are eternalists in whose view the substantiality of phenomena is accepted. However, no object whatsoever exists that is devoid of direction [dimension] and time [consciousness]. If you were to analyze the forms of direction and space, you could not possibly find a single entity that is not reducible to its component parts. And if a single entity does not exist, how could many appear? As there is no existence other than these, the conceptualization of existence is an inferior one.

Just as there is no length without shortness, how could a nature of nonexistence be apprehended when even a nature of existence is not obtained?

Know, intelligent one, that the real also does not consist of both existence and nonexistence because this possibility has been removed by the rejection of each individually; nor does it consist of being neither of these two, because there is no logical proof for this possibility, and, in any case, there is no possible bothness to which this could be an alternative.

But if we were to conclude that mind alone is real since it is formless and thus has no directions, we would have to admit that it also becomes plural and false if subject and object are identical [the latter being manifold].

If, however, subject and object are different from one another, then how do objects become objectified and mind subjectified? If the two arise dually, in what way [for example, simultaneously or otherwise] do they appear? Finally, what kind of liberation is achieved merely by rejecting illusory external appearances?

Since the object is not established as real by nature, the subject, too, is not established as real. The claim that there exists somehow a pure consciousness apart from these two is as extremely wrong as the Sāṃkhya philosophers' notion of a self [*puruṣa*] distinct from the transformations of primal nature [*prakṛti*].

Be free from supports, knowing that all phenomena from the first are unarisen, natureless, away from extremes, and like space.

Marvelous and much more wondrous than any wonder is this knowledge that does not relinquish the emptiness of all dharmas nor stop the process of interdependent origination!

Realize that objects are the nonduality of appearance and emptiness, that mind is the nonduality of knowledge and emptiness, and that the path to liberation is the nonduality of method and wisdom.

Finally, act [in accord with this insight].

The stages of cause, path, and result should be understood thus: the interdependent origination of the relative sphere is like illusion; in the ultimate, the nature of dharmas is emptiness; finally, both are nondual and without differentiation.

Thus if the foundation [morality], preparation [reflection], meditation, conclusion [dedication of merit and recollection], and the process of practice taken as a whole is each multiplied by three [in correspondence to the three stages of cause, path, and result], all the paths of virtue are gathered together in fifteen factors.

Whoever strives to perfect these factors in each performance of virtue enjoys the happiness of fortunate states and accumulates oceans of the two collections of merit and transcendent wisdom.

Through the clarity of his meditation, he becomes joined with the Āryan path and increases in transcendent wisdom as a result of his meditation and noble conduct. Then, attaining the goal [of buddhahood] through coursing along the final stages of the path, he puts an end to all thought constructions by realizing the nature of mind to be pure from the very beginning. His mind becomes one flavor with the *dharmadhātu* and is transformed into the *svābhāvikakāya*, which is the transcendent wisdom of dharmadhātu and the knowledge of the perfection of renunciation.

For him, the dharmas of worldly existence become transformed through the practice of the path so that his body becomes the body of an enlightened one adorned by 112 marks and signs of perfection; his voice becomes the voice of a buddha endowed with sixty tones; his mind is transformed into transcendent wisdom and is also endowed with omniscience. Passions are transformed into the boundless virtues of the conqueror and constitute the *saṃbhogakāya*. His deeds are transformed into the task accomplishing wisdom and the countless kinds of enlightened activity that form the *nirmāṇakāya*.

These five wisdoms constitute the perfect realization of the enlightened one, and, inasmuch as he is also endowed with spiritual power, they are unending and uninterrupted. May you also, O emperor, become like him!

Through the merit of offering this gift of Dharma
Which summarizes the deep sense of the noble path,
May all living beings with you, O king, as their chief,
Quickly attain the highest stage of enlightenment.

My own mind, too, has become encouraged
By composing these lines as a gift of doctrine
And so I shall speak further of another matter:
Undistractedly hear it, O lord among beings!

The time when you should make efforts is now:
Make firm the good fortune you have,
Ensure long life and the success of your lineage
And practice right methods to gain liberation.

It is right to make efforts without distraction.
At a time when Dharma has not yet set like a sun
And a religious king like yourself sits on the throne,
How can your mind remain indifferent to the plight
Of those who wear saffron robes?

Though I am not old, the strength of my body is slight
And my mind inclines to be lazy;
Therefore, I wish to be excused for a while
That I may seek Dharma's meaning in solitude.

3. Teaching on *A Gift of Dharma to Kublai Khan*

His Holiness Kyabgon Gongma Sakya
Trichen Rinpoche

Introduction: Creating the Right Motivation

Whenever you receive teachings, the first thing that you should do is create the right motivation. Receiving teachings with the wrong motivation is like receiving the wrong medical treatment for an illness—it will cause more problems than benefits. If you have greed or anger, for example, then it will be very harmful. If you don't have any particular motivation, or if you are merely curious, wanting to know more about the subject and treating it as general knowledge, it will not be of much benefit to you. If, however, you have the right motivation, then even a single line of teaching will be of tremendous benefit.

Right motivation has many levels. Whether we are Buddhists or non-Buddhists, whether we are human beings or some other kind of sentient being, we all wish to be free from suffering and have happiness. In fact, everyone—every individual, every society, and every country—is running one after another for the sake of overcoming their suffering and achieving happiness. However, real happiness cannot be had unless we change our minds.

Many people receive teachings in order to overcome suffering in this life, things such as physical pain, mental anxiety, legal problems, family problems, or relationship problems. There is great suffering in saṃsāra, or the worldly cycle of existence, and people seek spiritual help so that they can fulfill their worldly wishes for good health, a long life, prosperity, and so on. Although this is certainly a good motivation to have, it is still within the worldly cycle of existence and therefore is not the proper motivation for receiving the teachings. As it is said in *Parting from the Four Attachments*, the famous teaching given by Mañjuśrī to Sachen Kunga Nyingpo, "If you have attachment to this life, you are not a Dharmic or religious person."

To be considered Dharmic, one's motivation should at least be for results in the next life. After all, a human lifetime is very short. People almost never live to be even one hundred years old, and whatever you might gain or acquire in life—fame, prosperity, or success—has no lasting benefit. Therefore, although it is very important for us, as ordinary persons, to have a good life, it is not worth being attached to it. Life is like a bubble that floats on the surface of water. It can burst at any moment. Therefore receiving the teachings for the sake of this life is not a proper motivation.

Then again, many people receive teachings realizing that life is impermanent and that sooner or later we all must leave this world. When we die, our physical bodies will be disposed of in one way or another, but consciousness cannot be disposed of in the same way as the body. The invisible mind cannot be destroyed like the physical body; consciousness will continue. According to the teachings, the deeds that we commit determine where we will go when our mental consciousness continues. Virtuous deeds will lead consciousness into the higher realms, and negative deeds will lead consciousness into the lower realms. If one falls into one of the three lower realms—the hell realm, the hungry ghost realm, or the animal realm—there one will find tremendous suffering. I am sure that many of you are already familiar with the descriptions of the sufferings that are experienced there. There is no way to bear such suffering. After all, we cannot bear the suffering that we experience in this world, so how could we possibly bear the sufferings of the lower realms?

Wishing to be saved from the lower realms and wishing to be reborn again and again in the higher realms may be a very good motivation, but it is still within the circle of saṃsāra. Although one will not encounter as much suffering if one is born into a higher realm, there is still suffering. Without examination, we feel that in the higher realms there is a mixture of suffering with happiness, but in reality the higher realms are also full of nothing but suffering; the things that seem like happiness are only a more subtle kind of suffering. For this reason, it is not worth having any attachment to the cycle of existence. As it is said in *Parting from the Four Attachments*, "If you have attachment to the cycle of existence, you do not have proper renunciation." Proper renunciation means realizing that the higher realms also contain great suffering. If one carefully examines the whole of saṃsāra, one will find that there is not a single spot worthy of attachment.

With this kind of renunciation though, you might seek to completely renounce all of saṃsāra, seeing the entire cycle of existence to be like a burning fire or a nest of poisonous snakes, and then seek nirvāṇa or personal liberation. This, of course, is a very good thing. It is a very good motivation. However, you must then carefully think that there are innumerable other sentient beings in saṃsāra. If we believe in reincarnation—that we have had innumerable lives before now and that we will be born again and again in the future unless we attain liberation or enlightenment—then it follows that there is not a single place where one has not been born before, and there is not a single sentient being who has not at one time or another been one's own kind and loving parent. Abandoning all of them and seeking final liberation just for oneself alone is a very selfish thought.

If your close family members—your parents, brothers, sisters, children, partner—were in a miserable place experiencing great suffering while you were in a safe and happy place, then you wouldn't feel satisfied, assuming that you are a goodhearted person. You would rather be with your loved ones, so that at least you might share their miseries, regardless of whether or not you could really help them.

Well, just as space has no limit, sentient beings have no limit, and each sentient being is actually none other than our very dear father, mother, brother, sister, and so on. Each has given us much love and much care and protection, and each has benefited us in many ways. However, due to our change in birth we do not realize this, and we do not recognize each other. We view some people as enemies, some as friends, and some indifferently, when in reality every single sentient being is our very dear mother. This includes our most hated enemies, who today might be very harmful to us and seem very evil to us. They appear to us in the form of enemies, asking for the debts that we owe them because we did not pay back their kindness. Because every sentient being is our own dear mother, we must think of their well-being, their suffering, their benefit, and their happiness.

All sentient beings have the intention to overcome suffering and find lasting happiness, but in their ignorance they run on and on creating more suffering for themselves. They destroy the causes of their happiness because they lack wisdom. We must help them, but how can we do this? We are also ordinary people, and we do not have full knowledge, full compassion, or full power. We are completely bound by our karma and our defilements. Wherever the winds of karma blow, we have no choice but to go there. We cannot choose the form of our birth, and we cannot choose where we are born. How can we help other sentient beings?

We must begin by generating loving-kindness and compassion and the thought of benefiting all beings beyond what even the most powerful worldly deities like Brahmā, Viṣṇu, and Indra are able to do. Although they are very powerful, they are not able to help all sentient beings achieve freedom from suffering. They do not even have the thought of rescuing all sentient beings from the suffering of saṃsāra. Similarly, those who are in nirvāṇa, the śrāvakas and *pratyekabuddhas*, also do not have the power to save sentient beings. Only fully enlightened buddhas possess the knowledge, compassion, and ability to liberate all sentient beings from suffering.

When you attain buddhahood, you will be able to save countless sentient beings in just a single moment. Therefore your highest goal should be to attain buddhahood, not just for your own sake but also for the sake of all sentient beings, so that you can rescue them from the suffering of saṃsāra and bring them to a place of happiness. This should be your goal, and this is the highest motivation for receiving the teachings.

Because this is such an important and noble motivation, just having the idea in one's mind, the thought itself, is a great merit. All other things, such as our wishes for a long life, good health, and prosperity, are very small by comparison. In any case, when you have this noblest of motivations, all those mundane wishes will naturally be accomplished as well.

Right conduct is also important when receiving teachings. It is said in the sūtras that when you receive teachings you should be like a patient receiving advice from a doctor. When we are physically ill, of course, we rely carefully on our doctors' advice, and right now we are all sick with defilements. They are very strong, and they control our minds. We have no choice but to go in the direction in which our defilements lead us. We need a cure for this affliction. See the master who is giving the teachings as the doctor, see the Dharma as the medicine, and see oneself as the patient. See the act of receiving the teachings as receiving treatment, and see those who surround you as medical assistants.

Main Teaching: The Preliminaries

Now we turn to the teaching itself. All teachings and texts are divided into three parts: preliminaries, main part, and conclusion. So we start with the preliminaries, and the first preliminary is the *homage*. The homage serves three purposes. First, by paying homage to the Buddha, the guru, and whomever else is worthy of respect, an author shows that he is practicing holy conduct and demonstrates his intention to compose the text in the right way. Second, paying homage to the Buddha helps the author complete the text without obstacles. Finally, whenever one pays homage to the Buddha, one creates great merit, and whenever a reader reads the homage, he or she also gains great merit. The homage, as it is translated into English, is this:

> **To the incomparable enlightened one, who is endowed with the splendor of fame in name and the splendor of wondrous virtues (*yönten*) in actual fact, I offer homage.**

The Buddha is he who possesses both the splendor of renown as well as the actual good qualities of an enlightened being: "the splendor of wondrous virtues in actual fact." Beings like śrāvakas and pratyekabuddhas have virtues and a certain amount of the splendor of virtues, but they do not have the fame that buddhas have. Worldly deities such as Brahmā, Śiva, and Viṣṇu are very powerful and famous, but they lack the actual wondrous qualities that a buddha possesses. The Buddha is above both these classes of beings because only buddhas both are described as possessing wondrous virtues and actually possess them.

"Wondrous virtues" refers to the fact that buddhas have departed from all forms of obscurations—from the obscurations that are defilements and from the obscurations that obscure knowledge. They have departed from these obscurations themselves and also from their propensities. They have done so permanently, and they will never acquire them again. They have gained the great qualities that arise from knowing both *relative* and *absolute* truth. Such qualities are unique to the Buddha, and they are not shared by worldly deities or by śrāvakas and pratyekabuddhas. Thus the author's homage is to the Buddha or the enlightened one.

After paying homage to the Buddha, the author resolves to write the text and explains the purpose for writing the text. He says:

> **Although you, noble emperor, already know the discourses on worldly and spiritual science, still, as with the songs and music of musicians to which you listen again and again even when you have heard them all before, why shouldn't a poet repeat wise words?**

The Tibetan word here for "emperor" is a general term for someone who rules a country. He is referred to as "noble," indicating that he is a special ruler. In particular, he is an emperor who practices the holy Dharma and who follows holy conduct, and it is to such a Dharmic emperor that Chögyal Phagpa is going to explain this precious teaching.

But Kublai Khan has already encountered many virtuous Dharma friends and teachers, and he has already received many profound and vast teachings. What is the purpose of giving him more teachings on the Dharma? This is the doubt to be dispelled. As it says, even though Kublai Khan is learned in both worldly and spiritual matters, there is nothing wrong with explaining the Dharma to him again. For example, we listen to music for the sake of enjoyment even when we have heard the same songs many times. Similarly, Chögyal Phagpa, writing in verse, asks, "Why shouldn't a poet repeat wise words?"

But unlike this example, these words are not meant only for enjoyment. Through the Dharma, one can overcome the suffering of saṃsāra, and this is an extraordinarily great purpose and a great benefit. It is worthwhile to remember it and to enhance one's knowledge of it, and this is the twofold purpose for giving the teaching.

Think of a beautiful palace made entirely of white marble. It is already beautiful, but if it reflects the light of the full moon, then it will become even more beautiful, and its whiteness will appear with greater clarity. Similarly, the emperor may already know many profound teachings, but repeating them will enhance his knowledge. His knowledge will grow and become clearer like the palace of marble in the light of the full moon.

Enhancement and remembrance, however, are only temporary purposes. As I have already said, the ultimate goal or motivation is to attain full enlightenment and then to help all sentient beings. And we do this by hearing the teachings again and again and so gaining ever deeper understanding.

> **All the countless teachings of Dharma taught by the sage for the sake of countless disciples indeed are meant to be practiced. But how may this be done?**

"Sage" refers to the Buddha, whose excellent qualities of body, voice, and enlightened mind enabled him to give countless teachings. Because sentient beings are countless and have different mentalities, intentions, propensities, tastes, and defilements, the Buddha gave innumerable teachings to help them. In Sanskrit, the teaching is called the Dharma. We can split the word *dharma* into its two syllables, *dhar* and *ma*. In Sanskrit, *dhara* means "holding" and *manas* means "mind." Thus dharma is "mind-holding."

All phenomena are divisible into two categories, the *conventional* and the *absolute*. At the conventional, or relative, level, each dharma—*dharma* here means phenomenon—has its own distinguishing characteristics. Because they possess these specific characteristics we are able to differentiate entities. But if we carefully examine the matter—if we look at them on the absolute level—phenomena do not really possess these characteristics. By fully knowing the two truths of the relative and the absolute, we will be able to hold our minds—and hold firm against falling into saṃsāra.

The Dharma has no limit, although there are certain numbers that we speak of, such as when we refer to the 84,000 teachings of the Buddha. These numbers are not the actual numbers of the teachings that the Buddha gave. Instead, they are the numbers of teachings that the Buddha's various disciples received. Ānanda, for example, received 84,000 teachings, and that is where this number originates. The actual teachings of the Buddha have no limit. Remember that limitless sentient beings have a limitless variety of ideas and propensities, and the Buddha gave teachings to suit every kind and every level of being.

These limitless teachings are not meant to be merely studied and debated. They are meant to be *practiced*. This is the purpose for which the Buddha taught them, and if we do not practice the teachings, their purpose is not realized. Whatever knowledge you may have gained, whatever teaching you may have received, whether large or small, the point of it is that you might practice it. When you take the teaching into your daily life and you make it a part of your practice, only then will it have served its purpose.

There are many ways to divide the teachings. Generally, we refer to the three *yānas*. *Yāna* means "vehicle" or way to get to one's destination. The three yānas are the Śrāvakayāna, the Pratyekabuddhayāna, and the Bodhisattvayāna. We are followers of the Buddhist Mahāyāna, which is the same as the Bodhisattvayāna.

In the Bodhisattvayāna we are followers of the *bodhisattva vow*. Bodhisattvas are said to be "sons of the Buddha." This is a way of saying that entering the bodhisattva path ensures that you will become a buddha in the future, in the same way that the child will carry on the parent's name. In the Śrāvakayāna and the Pratyekabuddhayāna, on the other hand, the ultimate goal is not to become a buddha but instead to become an arhat.

One might think that since the Buddha gave innumerable teachings on the Pratyekabuddhayāna and the Śrāvakayāna, and since every teaching is meant to be practiced, we should also practice the Śrāvakayāna and the Pratyekabuddhayāna teachings. Certainly this is so. The Śrāvakayāna and Pratyekabuddhayāna teachings mainly explain how to abstain from physical and verbal wrongdoing. The bodhisattva precepts are mainly to abstain from mental wrongdoing. The bodhisattva precepts also include abstinence from physical and verbal wrongdoings as well, though, so there is no contradiction. Every teaching is to be practiced, including the Śrāvakayāna and Pratyekabuddhayāna teachings, and because a bodhisattva's *motivation* is to attain full enlightenment, or buddhahood, all of the practices that he does—even those of the lower yānas—become for him the path to buddhahood.

Finally, in the Vajrayāna, when we take the precepts of the five buddha families (Amitābha, Akṣobhya, Ratnasambhava, Amoghasiddhi, and Vairocana), the Buddha Amitābha's precept is to practice every teaching of the Buddha—the teachings of the three yānas and of the four classes of tantra. Moreover, when you attain enlightenment, you will need to give the teachings of all three yānas. In order to give such teachings, you must know them and practice them. Otherwise you will not be able to show the correct path to sentient beings.

How to Practice the Teachings: The Five Topics

How then do we practice? How may this be done? Up to this point we have considered the preliminaries, and here begins the main part of the teaching. *How to practice* has five topics:

1. Pure moral discipline as the foundation of the path
2. Motivating factors as the prelude to the path
3. The yoga of meditation as the core of the path
4. Subsequent efforts and methods for deepening the virtues of the path
5. Infusion of all the paths and elements of the Dharma

1. Pure Moral Discipline as the Foundation of the Path

Just as the earth is the base of everything animate and inanimate, and without the earth we could not stand, pure moral conduct is the foundation upon which all the qualities arise. The manner in which one is to practice pure moral conduct is given through an example:

> **A subject, bound by fear and a sense of shame, does not disobey his king's command but dwells in right conduct without harming others and, as a result, grows in good fortune and even earns the praises of the king. It is similar with a person who**

accepts, in accordance with his ability to accomplish them, the rules of discipline enjoined by the sage to help beginners on the Śrāvakayāna and Mahāyāna paths.

In ancient times, every country had a king, and every person was bound to the king through fear of punishment. To go against a powerful king might bring very severe punishment. Out of this fear and out of a sense of shame that if one breaks the rules one would be criticized or censured, one kept the law of the king or queen of one's country.

One could also obtain good fortune by keeping the law of the king. Your wealth and lineage would increase. The king would praise you, and you might receive awards, medals, and so on. If you received honors or recognition from the king, then naturally the ministers and others would find you praiseworthy, too.

This is the example. At the worldly level, of course it is useful to obey the laws of the king of your country—you will have nothing to fear, and you will gain name, fame, prosperity, and praise.

If after properly receiving vows from an abbot, that person guards them from a fear of seen and unseen sufferings in worldly existence and from a sense of shame when he reflects, "The multitudes of noble ones who know the thoughts of other beings will be shamed if I break my vows. . . ."

As a base for one's practice, pure moral discipline is very important. Just as the earth is the foundation for all animate and inanimate things, pure moral discipline is the foundation for developing all good qualities. This has three parts: the *prātimokṣa* vow, the *bodhisattva* vow, and the *Mantrayāna* vows.

The great Lord Buddha, who possesses infinite wisdom, compassion, and power, through his skillful means has bestowed an enormous number of teachings. Therefore there are different levels of vows for practitioners at different levels of ability. When the Buddha lived in India, the majority of his disciples were followers of the Śrāvakayāna and the Pratyekabuddhayāna. For this general audience, the Buddha emphasized the teachings of these lower yānas. Most beings are unable to follow the higher path; "beginners on the Śrāvakayāna and Mahāyāna paths" refers to these general followers of the Buddha. The Buddha wished to help them, and so in order to benefit these practitioners of the Śrāvakayāna and Pratyekabuddhayāna, the Buddha gave the prātimokṣa or the individual liberation vows.

The prātimokṣa, or individual liberation, vow is mainly for purifying physical and verbal wrongdoings. Most of the rules in it are to abstain from physical and verbal negative deeds. This is easier to do than abstaining from mental wrongdoing, and that is why it is emphasized in the common yānas.

There are many different levels of vows and precepts. The very first is called the *refuge precept*. Without taking refuge, you cannot receive any other vows. In fact, if you do not take refuge, then you are not even Buddhist. Being born into a Buddhist family does not make you a Buddhist. It is only when you go for refuge that you become a Buddhist, whether your family is Buddhist or not. More specifically, you must take refuge in the Buddha, Dharma, and Saṅgha for the sake of liberation. If you take refuge for the sake of worldly purposes, this is not proper refuge. Proper refuge should at least be for the sake of liberation.

After taking refuge—becoming a Buddhist—then you can receive further vows. Basically there are these three: the *upāsaka*, the *śrāmaṇera*, and the *bhikṣu* vows. Upāsaka vows are layperson's vows. There is no difference between the upāsaka vows for men and for women. The only distinctions are according to one's ability. Ideally, every Buddhist should keep all five of the upāsaka precepts, the *pañcaśīla*: to abstain from killing, lying, stealing, sexual misconduct, and intoxication. However, if you cannot keep them all, then you can take just one or two precepts, but only when you make a vow to keep all five is one called an upāsaka.

If you vow to abstain from killing living beings, you must abstain from killing any living being whatsoever from insects on up. If you kill a being accidentally—for example, by stepping on an insect—this does not count as breaking the vow because there was no intention to kill. To break the vow, there must be these four factors present: a base, an intention, an action, and the ultimate. The base means a being other than you—another being, from an insect up to a human. There must also be an intention to kill. The rules are very specific. If you have a wish to kill somebody, for example, and then you do it but through an accident—in some kind of mistake—this does not completely meet the criteria because you did not have the intention. The action is, for example, stabbing or giving poison. If the living being then becomes dead as a result, this is called the ultimate or the outcome.

Higher than upāsaka is the śrāmaṇera, which means "novice." This is someone in preparation for the higher vows of monks and nuns, called the bhikṣu and *bhikṣuṇī* precepts respectively. The different levels of vows meet the needs of practitioners at different levels of ability, and one should only take vows according to one's ability.

To summarize, the first level is the refuge precept holder. After that, there are the one-precept, two-precept, three-precept, four-precept, and five-precept holders. If one keeps all five, this is the full upāsaka vow for laypeople. At a higher level, if you wish to enter the monastic life, you can choose to take the śrāmaṇera vow, which is for monks as well as for nuns. And after that, you can receive the bhikṣu or the bhikṣuṇī vows, which are the highest level of vow according to the prātimokṣa.

Vows should be properly received from an abbot. Upāsaka vows can be received from one person, for example, from one's preceptor. The śrāmaṇera and the bhikṣu and bhikṣuṇī vows must be received from an abbot as well as the saṅgha or a group of monks or nuns. They should be received with the proper ritual, at the proper time, and in the proper place. Then, after you properly receive the vows, the abbot will guide you in keeping them. If you can keep the vows, you can experience great benefit.

At the worldly level, people obey laws from a fear of punishment and from a sense of shame or modesty. Likewise, if you do not keep the vows, you will experience the fear of "seen and unseen suffering in worldly existence." Suffering that is seen means suffering in this life. You will encounter great suffering if you do not keep the vows. "Unseen" means that in the future you will experience the great sufferings of the three lower realms—the hell realm, the hungry ghost realm, and the animal realm—depending upon your defilement. For example, if you kill somebody out of anger or hatred, you will most likely be born in the hell realm. If you kill out of greed—killing animals for their flesh, skins, or bones, for example—then most likely you will be born in the hungry ghost realm. Some people kill out of ignorance, for the sake of fun or sport. And in some countries, animals are sacrificed in religious rituals. Such deeds can cause you to be born as an animal. If you must experience these sufferings of birth in the lower realms, then of course there is no way to bear it. So from our fear of suffering we will keep the vows.

We also keep them out of a sense of shame. Although you can hide from ordinary people and pretend that you are not breaking any rules, the buddhas and bodhisattvas have full omniscience, and you cannot hide your misdeeds from them. Whatever you do, buddhas and bodhisattvas will see you as clearly as you can see your own palm.

Keeping the vows brings tremendous benefit. You will gain joy in worldly existence, and, more important, you will gain the qualities of perfect liberation.

> **Then, as a result, he will become a foundation not only of seen and unseen joys in worldly existence but also of the virtues of perfect liberation. He will also become a worthy object of veneration for men and gods and even receive the praises of buddhas.**

As before, "seen" refers to results in this life: if you abstain from killing, you will have a long life, and if you abstain from stealing, you will have wealth. "Unseen joys" means that in the next life you will be born into the higher realms. For instance, a large amount of virtue will lead to rebirth in the god realm. Middling virtue will bring rebirth in the demigod realm, and a small amount will lead to rebirth in the human realm. There, you will enjoy all the qualities of the higher realms, such as long life, good health, wealth, power, wisdom, a good body, and so on. These are called the seven qualities of the higher realms.

More important, if you keep good discipline, if you avoid doing wrong things, which cause regrets to come with them, then your mind will become calm. Wrongdoing causes the mind to be disturbed—you feel regrets, or you have a guilty feeling. When the mind is disturbed in this way, you cannot have good experience with meditation. However, if you keep the vows, you will not experience regret or guilt, and your mind will become very calm. As a result, you can do calm-abiding meditation, also called *concentration* or *śamatha*. Then when your mind becomes very calm and steady, and can remain in the single-pointedness of śamatha, you can cultivate insight wisdom, or *vipaśyanā*. You will be able to control the mind and change the mind, and you will be able to gain complete liberation from saṃsāra.

All of us realize that the defilements, or negative emotions, are very harmful to us. They harm us physically and mentally. They harm us in this life and in the next. But because we have been associated with the defilements for such a long period of time, it is very difficult to stop them. The only way to change is through meditation. Through meditation, we can change our minds. This was the Buddha's purpose in giving teachings. This is not easy, of course. It is extremely difficult to meditate, even for a single moment. You must be in a secluded place, and many other factors must be met. Most of all, it is important that your mind be calm.

At the moment we do not have freedom because our defilements are very strong and they control our minds. Because of their strong power, we cannot practice and we cannot do the right things. But through meditation we can. Therefore keeping the prātimokṣa vows is very beneficial. In addition, if you keep the vows you will become a worthy object of veneration for men and gods. You will even receive the praise of the Buddha. Many quotations from the sūtras support this point.

This explains why the lower yānas, the śrāvaka and pratyekabuddha precepts, pertain mostly to physical and verbal actions; they are easier to control than the mind. It is easy to abstain from killing and stealing, but it is very difficult to avoid negative emotions arising in the mind. Therefore Buddha has explained for beginners and for general followers the way to tame physical and verbal conduct. Next, the bodhisattva vows were taught in order to control our minds, and also in order to benefit not just ourselves but other sentient beings as well.

These three realms of existence, after all, are just suffering, while nirvāṇa, too, is just peace. Looking with pity, therefore,

> **on those who wish either for worldly existence or nirvāṇa, the Buddha alone, himself free from sorrow, removes sorrow, and, having himself attained great joy, bestows joy. And he has appeared from among beings like us.**

This explains the first two causes of *bodhicitta*, the enlightenment mind: compassion and the desire to attain buddhahood.

The universe is divided into three realms—the realm of desire, the realm of forms, and the realm of formlessness. The *kāmadhātu*, or realm of desire, is where we are residing. It has six different realms within it, three lower and three higher. The three lower are the hell realm, the hungry ghost realm, and the animal realm, and the three higher are the human realm, the demigod realm, and the god realm. The kāmadhātu is where beings who indulge in passions remain, and it said to be a place of both the cause and the result of suffering. Higher than the kāmadhātu is the *rūpadhātu*, the realm of forms, and higher than the rūpadhātu is the *arūpadhātu*, the formless realm. In these two realms, there is no visible suffering as we see in the realm of desire. And although there is no actual indulgence of the passions in these states, one still remains with the causes of suffering: beings that dwell there have the causes of suffering but not the result.

Generally speaking, there are three kinds of suffering: the suffering of suffering, the suffering of change, and the suffering due to the conditional nature of phenomena. The suffering of suffering means suffering that we normally consider to be suffering—things such as physical pain, mental anxiety, and so on. The suffering of change refers to what we normally consider to be pleasures or joys. Although something may appear as joy or pleasure, in reality it is another form of suffering. Even though you enjoy it at the moment, there is apprehension in the knowledge that this will change, that this will become suffering again. The suffering of the conditional nature of all phenomena means that everything is impermanent. All compounded things are impermanent, and what is impermanent is suffering. Thus the entirety of saṃsāra—whether it is the realm of desire, the realm of forms, or the formless realm—is everywhere actually suffering. Even if you reach the pinnacle of existence in saṃsāra, this state will not be permanent. You will fall, and you will have to experience great suffering again. There is not a single spot that is worthy of attachment. Saṃsāra is full of suffering, and there is nothing in it worthy of attachment.

On the other side, we have the nirvāṇa of the śrāvakas and pratyekabuddhas. Since they do not have suffering, one might think that one should try to attain nirvāṇa. Of course, it is true that compared to saṃsāra nirvāṇa is a very good thing. But while the so-called small nirvāṇas or medium nirvāṇas of the śrāvakas and pratyekabuddhas do not have gross suffering, they still have subtle obscurations, and there are still propensities for ignorance. Attaining nirvāṇa does not mean you have developed your full qualities. Moreover, it becomes the greatest obstacle to attaining full enlightenment. For these reasons, it is not worthy.

At one time, Śāriputra was preparing to deliver a discourse on the Dharma. Through hearing him, every one of the five hundred disciples in the audience would attain arhatship or nirvāṇa. However, just before he began, the bodhisattva Mañjuśrī appeared and, because Mañjuśrī was senior to Śāriputra and a great bodhisattva, Śāriputra requested Mañjuśrī to give the discourse instead. All the people who received teachings from Mañjuśrī that day fell into the hell realm. Śāriputra went to the Buddha to inform him of this, saying, "Today Mañjuśrī did something very wrong." Buddha asked him, "What did he do?" Śāriputra explained, "I was about to give teachings, and had I done so the listeners would, each one, have attained the stage of an arhat. But I asked Mañjuśrī to give the teachings in my place, and as a consequence all the listeners fell into the hell realm." Buddha said, "What Mañjuśrī did was the right thing. If you had given the teachings and they had attained arhatship, they would have remained in that state for an inconceivable duration. It would have become the greatest obstacle to their attaining enlightenment. However, Mañjuśrī gave the teaching and so they fell into the hell realm temporarily—a quick ripening of whatever negative deeds remained. They suffer now, but soon they will be free from the hell realm. They will enter into the bodhisattva path, and they will attain enlightenment very quickly. Therefore what Mañjuśrī did was the right thing."

From the bodhisattva's point of view, on the one side there is saṃsāra, full of suffering and faults, and on the other side there is nirvāṇa, or complete peace and the cessation of suffering. Both are extremes. Both are objects of compassion. Saṃsāra has so much obvious suffering, physically and mentally, that even ordinary persons can see this and feel strong pity and great compassion. In nirvāṇa, although beings do not have any gross suffering as such, they still have not gained great bliss. It will take an unimaginable amount of time for them to attain full enlightenment. Therefore it is also an object of compassion.

The first cause of creating the enlightenment mind, then, is compassion. When you enter the bodhisattva path, every practice that you do is not for your own sake but for the sake of all sentient beings. To achieve this, the first thing you need is genuine compassion. We all have a certain amount of compassion, but at the moment our compassion is very limited. We have compassionate feelings for friends and family. It is easy for love to arise for them, but it is very limited. It is not genuine compassion, which means compassion for all sentient beings irrespective of whether they are friends or enemies, relatives or strangers. It includes our most hated enemies. It means compassion and love for everyone, without any exception and without any distinction. This includes the noble ones residing in nirvāṇa. We must develop compassion for both extremes of saṃsāra and nirvāṇa, and this is the first cause of creating the enlightenment mind. So it is said, "Looking with pity, therefore, on those who wish either for worldly existence or nirvāṇa. . . ."

The second cause of the enlightenment mind is having buddhahood for our goal. "The Buddha alone, himself free from sorrow, removes sorrow." We must have buddhahood for our goal, also called *nonabiding nirvāṇa* or the *great nirvāṇa*. "Nonabiding" means not residing in either of the extremes. Since the Buddha has departed from all forms of obscuration, he is completely free from any kind of suffering or obscuration.

He is also able to bestow joy. The Buddha has physical, verbal, and mental activities, and innumerable other qualities, but the most important of these is his verbal activity. It is by giving teachings that he helps others to remove their sorrows. This is how he bestows joy. The Buddha, himself departed from all forms of obscurations, gives great bliss by giving teachings. According to Buddhist teachings, the Buddha is great not because he performed great miracles and saves beings—though there are, of course, such stories and instances—but rather because he helps sentient beings by giving teachings. We must practice the teachings, and through that we are saved. Therefore it said that you yourself are the savior of you. Nobody else can save you. Only you can save yourself by yourself. The Buddha said, "I have shown you the path to liberation, but liberation itself depends upon you." Liberation is not something that can be given by the Buddha like a gift. We must make efforts to achieve liberation and enlightenment. What we should aim for then is not the nirvāṇa of the śrāvakas and the pratyekabuddhas, but full enlightenment or buddhahood. Just as Buddha departed from all forms of obscurations and attained great bliss, so must we, too.

One might think that it is true that the Buddha is great and that we must attain buddhahood, but as ordinary persons with a lot of shortcomings, we might not be able to accomplish so great a result. To overcome this, we must recall what is said here: "He has appeared from among beings like ourselves." Buddha was not enlightened from the very beginning. He was an ordinary person with defilements and shortcomings like us. But he entered the bodhisattva path and he practiced. He made efforts. He accumulated the merit and wisdom heaps, and he departed from all forms of obscurations, the obscurations of defilements and the obscurations of knowledge. With that, he achieved enlightenment. There is no reason why we, too, cannot attain enlightenment.

Like the Buddha, many of the great mahāsiddhas and masters were just ordinary people in the beginning. Tibet's great yogi Milarepa was an ordinary man with many worldly problems and sufferings. But after meeting a great master and after undergoing a great deal of hardship in order to purify his negative deeds, he attained great realization. They were like us, and so we should not feel discouraged.

Furthermore, the text says:

> **We can use the methods he used. Without timidity and laziness, therefore, you should unwaveringly aspire to win highest enlightenment and feel free to think, "I must surely attain buddhahood."**

One must think that the Buddha has attained the great qualities of liberation from all obscurations and accomplishment of ultimate realization, and that we can do the same. Naturally, doubts or questions will arise. For example, the obscurations are mixed together so thoroughly with our minds—is it even possible to eliminate them? If it can be done, how? And even if one could eliminate them, wouldn't one simply reacquire them, like the dirt of the body? We wash our bodies and take daily baths, but we become dirty again, day after day. These three kinds of questions arise.

The answer is that the obscurations are not in the nature of the mind. If they were, we would not be able to completely eliminate them. The nature of coal is to be black, and no matter how much you wash coal, it will never become white. The nature of the mind is clear light. It is never stained with obscurations, and therefore it is possible to eliminate them forever.

When the causes are gone, the obscurations will not reappear. The main cause of the obscurations—the source of all the defilements and all faults—is ignorance, or lack of wisdom, and the antidote is to gain wisdom. *Ignorance* here means "self-clinging." We cling to self without logical reasons for doing so, and due to this the other negative emotions arise. The direct antidote is the wisdom that realizes selflessness. With this, we eliminate the cause of the obscuration.

The first cause of the enlightenment mind is compassion. The second cause is the longing or great desire to attain buddhahood. The third is to proceed without timidity or laziness.

One should not feel timid, thinking that it takes such a long period of time to attain buddhahood, or thinking that one must go through great hardships, or despairing that one must work for countless numbers of sentient beings or learn innumerable teachings. All of this may seem very difficult. It is true, for example, that there is no limit to the number of sentient beings. However, it is actually only because sentient beings are limitless that one can accumulate the merit heap. If you generate compassion for one sentient being, it is difficult to accumulate very much merit, but if you generate compassion for limitless sentient beings, then you will acquire great merit quickly. In this way you can see that it is actually easier to accumulate vast merit because there are limitless sentient beings.

According to Mahāyāna teachings, those who have the best diligence and the best intelligence will require three countless eons in order to attain buddhahood. That is a very, very long period of time. However, if you consider that we are talking about such an extraordinary result as buddhahood, then this is not such a long time. And besides this, time is relative. For one person, what may be a very long period of time may for another person be very short. For certain bodhisattvas, a *kalpa*, or eon, passes like one week for an ordinary human, while for other beings a week can seem like an eon. As you go from bliss to bliss, from happiness to happiness, it will become easier to relinquish timidity. You should not be discouraged.

There are five paths that are stages on the path to buddahood: the path of accumulation, the path of application, the path of seeing, the path of meditation, and the path of no-more-learning. The first, the path of accumulation, is the path of bodhisattvas who are ordinary beings in the worldly level. When you create the enlightenment mind, you become a bodhisattva and you reach the path of accumulation. As you improve, you reach the path of application. This path is also within the worldly level, but it is nearer to the beyond-worldly level, so it is like the joint or transition between the worldly and the beyond-worldly levels. If one reaches the path of application, one will never fall again into the lower realms; one will have reached an irreversible state of progression. And when you reach the path of seeing, the third path, then you will never fall again to even the ordinary, wordly level. From there, you go only further and further through the path of meditation to the path of no-more-learning and buddhahood.

So therefore you should not be discouraged. The time that we have spent in saṃsāra is endless, countless; there is no such thing as a beginning to saṃsāra. From beginningless time until now we have been caught in saṃsāra and we have experienced innumerable sufferings. Compared to that, three countless eons is not a very long period of time.

So then there are three reasons or causes of the enlightenment mind: compassion, the intention to attain enlightenment, and encouragement. With these, you create the enlightenment mind and enter the bodhisattva path. When you realize how important it is for you to attain enlightenment, for your own sake and for the sake of others, when you think what great benefit is to be had, and when you have a strong wish to attain full enlightenment for the sake of all sentient beings, this is called *wishing enlightenment mind*. If you express this wish as a vow in front of your preceptor and all the buddhas and bodhisattvas, then it is called creating the wishing enlightenment mind. Next there is *entering enlightenment mind*. To achieve enlightenment, you cannot merely wish for it. You must make great efforts. You must enter the bodhisattva path; you must follow the footsteps of the great bodhisattvas. When you wish to follow the bodhisattva's way of life, to practice the six *pāramitās*, the four means of gathering, and so on, this is called *entering enlightenment mind*. If you create this mind or thought as a vow in front of the preceptors, buddhas, and bodhisattvas, then it is called *creating the entering enlightenment mind*.

You become a bodhisattva when you have generated enlightenment mind. Although you may be a completely ordinary person, and although you may be completely bound by your karma and defilements, when you generate the enlightenment mind you have the true name of bodhisattva, and you are already on the path of the bodhisattva.

The rules of the bodhisattva vow differ according to the level of the disciples, but the main rule is never to give up the wish to attain enlightenment. In order to achieve this, you must follow the path of the great bodhisattvas.

After the prātimokṣa and the bodhisattva vows, the third are the Vajrayāna vows.

> **Guard as your own life the vows you have made that, if violated, will cause you to be burned in hells, and that, if preserved, will enable you to experience truly wonderful results in proceeding from joy to joy even now.**

Here, the sequence in Tibetan and what you have in English are slightly different. This verse explains the Mantrayāna vows. Whenever buddhas appear in the universe it is called a *light eon*; if a buddha does not appear, it is called a *dark eon*. There are a great many dark eons and very few light eons. During the present eon, there are a thousand buddhas, and it is called a *fortunate eon*. And of all these thousand buddhas, none of them gives Mantrayāna teachings. They teach for the general audience, for general followers. The majority are followers of the Śrāvakayāna path or the Mahāyāna path, and they are not suitable to enter the Vajrayāna.

At present, only our Lord Śākyamuni Buddha, who from his special courage and special compassion attained enlightenment in this degenerate time, has the power to give the Mantrayāna teachings even to ordinary persons like us. The Mantrayāna teaching is very important. Those who have great diligence and wisdom and who practice the general Mahāyāna require three countless eons to attain enlightenment, which is a very long period of time. In the Vajrayāna, however, those who are fortunate and have great diligence and wisdom can attain enlightenment within one human lifetime. That is extremely short, extremely fast. Those who do not have such great diligence or fortune can still attain realization either at the time of death or in the bardo state, which is also extremely fast. Those who are inferior, who do not have such ability to attain results, if they have not committed the downfalls, will attain enlightenment within seven human lifetimes. This again is extremely fast. So the Vajrayāna vow and the Vajrayāna teachings are certainly very precious.

The Vajrayāna vows are explained here through four points, beginning with the consequences that you will face if you break the vows. If they are violated, you will be "burned in hells." That is the consequence. Vajrayāna vows are known as the samaya, and *samaya* means "time." From the moment that you receive the vows onward, you are bound by them. If you violate them, then you will be born in the lower realms—the hell realm, the hungry ghost realm, or the animal realm—where there is an unimaginable amount of suffering.

However, and this is the second point, if you keep the samaya then you will experience great benefit, "truly wonderful results in proceeding from joy to joy even now." Keep the vows intact and you will experience both the temporary and the ultimate result. Within this life, at the time of death, or within seven or sixteen lifetimes, you will be able to obtain the great result. If you keep the vows, this is the benefit that you will receive. "Even now" means the temporary result, proceeding from joy to joy.

The third point is that one must receive the Vajrayāna vows properly. This means receiving them from a qualified guru, in the right maṇḍala, at the right time, and through the right rituals.

Generally speaking, we distinguish between empowerments, blessings, and permissions. Receiving empowerment before beginning Mantrayāna practice is very important. Regarding major empowerments, there are different maṇḍalas for different persons or types of beings. For ordinary persons, there are only two kinds wherein you can receive the empowerment: sand maṇḍalas and painted maṇḍalas. When the guru is very advanced and the disciple is also at a high level, the empowerment can be received in a body maṇḍala or a meditational maṇḍala, but for an ordinary person there must be a physical representation, as well as a qualified guru and the proper rituals.

Most major empowerments require two days. The first day is just to test your ability, to discern whether or not you have a karmic connection to the Vajrayāna path, and if you do, to learn the kind of siddhis that you can acquire, and so on. This is done by throwing the tooth sticks, by observing your dreams, and so on. Then, on the second day, you receive the empowerment.

There are different kinds of empowerments for the four different classes of tantra: the *kriyā*, *caryā*, *yoga*, and *anuttarayoga* tantras. In the anuttarayoga tantra, there are actually four empowerments that are given. These are called the *vase*, *secret*, *wisdom*, and *fourth* empowerments.

The fourth point is that the Vajrayāna vows must be kept properly. In the English translation, this appears first: "Guard as your own life the vows you have made." Life is very precious, and similarly important are the samayas received during the empowerment. They are so precious that they should be guarded as you keep your own precious life.

Since the three sets of vows—of the Śrāvakayāna, Mahāyāna, and Vajrayāna paths—are the foundation whereon all virtues may arise, remain, and grow within oneself and others, try from the very first to be firm in their observance.

All three sets of vows—the prātimokṣa, the bodhisattva, and the samaya—are important because through keeping them all good qualities will arise, remain, and grow. On the basis of these sets of vows, all worldly and beyond-worldly qualities arise. In the meantime, for the practitioner, they are the foundation upon which these developing qualities remain. And from them also the qualities grow or increase to fruition. Therefore it says you must be firm in their observation. This completes the first part: pure moral discipline as the foundation of the path.

2. *Motivating Factors as the Prelude to the Path*

> **Become certain that the teaching, which is virtuous in its beginning, middle, and end, and whose words are quite flawless and not contradictory to the two logical proofs of valid knowledge, is the unique spiritual way among ways.**

The first motivating factor is faith. When we say "faith," we mean faith with wisdom; blind faith is not right. Why do we have faith in the Buddha? After all, every religion claims that its founder is the best, that their lord is the greatest and possesses all good qualities. Just saying that the Buddha is great does not prove anything. What we must do is prove for ourselves, individually, the greatness of the Buddha. His greatness is because of the teachings that he gave, and it is when we practice them, and as a result we gain good qualities and our minds change, that we can prove his greatness through our own experience.

In our Lamdré teachings, we talk about the four authenticities. These four can be explained in different orders, such as how it is written in the scriptures, how they are practiced, and so on. But the method to establish the four authenticities is first to study, then to contemplate, and then to meditate—and then you will gain experiences. When you gain authentic experiences as a result of first studying, then contemplating, and finally meditating, that is when you can establish that your guru is an authentic guru, the teachings that you have received from him are authentic teachings, and that they are based upon the Buddha's authentic sermons, his authentic teachings. It is in this way that we establish the four authenticities.

If we merely believe that the Buddha is great, if we have mere faith in the Buddha without cultivating any of our own experience based upon his teachings, then it will be difficult for us to have a strong inner conviction.

If someone were to say that there is some better teacher, then our minds might change at any time. However, when you have your own experience, then you will not be changeable.

The good qualities of the Buddha have no limit. He has qualities that no one can fully describe, even if one were to go on describing them for eons. Birds set off and fly in the sky, and if they return it is not because there is not enough space for them to keep going; it is because they exhaust their strength. Anyone who sets out to describe the Buddha's qualities would exhaust themselves because of the limits to their knowledge and ability. However, we indicate or summarize his good qualities as these three: wisdom, compassion, and power. The Buddha's wisdom means that his teachings are flawless; they have no fault and are not to be believed blindly. Buddha himself said that monks, nuns, and wise people should examine his teaching just as if they were buying gold, making sure that it is genuine. We cut, burn, and scratch the surface of gold, and only when we are convinced that it is genuine do we buy it. Likewise, the Buddha said of his own teachings that you should not just follow them by mere faith but only after examining them carefully for yourself using your own intelligence. Buddha never said, "You have to follow my teachings." This is why it says here, "not contradictory to the two logical proofs of valid knowledge."

The experience that you will gain is that the teachings are virtuous in the beginning, virtuous in the meantime, and virtuous in the end. They are virtuous in the beginning because when you hear the teachings they challenge your understanding of the defilements. In the beginning, most of us do not even realize that the defilements are harmful. Many people think that the defilements are actually good. They will say that someone is very brave, for example, or someone did this or that great thing. But in fact the defilements are the source of all suffering. The teachings of the Buddha challenge the defilements. Next, you contemplate what you have heard. This suppresses the defilements. They do not activate because of the time and effort spent in contemplation. Finally, you meditate. We change our minds and eliminate the defilements only through meditation.

Even though the Buddha has limitless knowledge or wisdom, if he did not also have compassion then he would not have given the teachings to others. So it says here:

> **Know, too, that the enlightened one who taught it is endowed with unhindered wisdom and great compassion since he revealed the truth without close-fistedness and with tremendous power.**

Without hiding anything, the Buddha gave profound and vast teachings from his great compassion. He is like a mother who has only one child. All mothers love their children, but mothers who have only one child have a special connection to that child. This is the manner in which the Buddha has compassion for all sentient beings, and this is why he gave the teachings.

Even though he has great knowledge and great compassion, if the Buddha lacked power, he would not be able to overcome obstacles or unfavorable conditions. But in fact the Buddha has tremendous power.

The very first step on the path is taking refuge in the Buddha, Dharma, and Saṅgha. Here the Dharma is discussed first. This is because when the teachings are described, we are able to understand immediately that the one who gave such teachings is a worthy object of refuge as well. It is a proof that the Buddha is great, and he becomes an object of refuge not only out of blind faith. This explains the Buddha and the Dharma together.

Next is the Saṅgha:

> **Because they are his followers and a gathering of beings with virtues similar to his, and because your own sphere of spiritual activity is identical to theirs, know the noble assembly of bodhisattvas to be the best field for increasing your merit.**

The first importance of the Saṅgha is that they are not followers of worldly deities. They are followers of the Buddha. Second, although they do not have the full qualities of the Buddha, they have qualities similar to his, and their activities are the same. We take the Saṅgha as our companions on the path—"know the noble assembly of bodhisattvas to be the best field for increasing your merit." We take the Buddha as the guide who can show us the correct path, and the Dharma as the path itself because we must practice the Dharma in order to reach our destination. It is not enough to have a good guide; you must actually walk or travel the path yourself. You must practice the Dharma to attain enlightenment. The Saṅgha are your traveling companions on the path. Instead of traveling alone, you have companions. In this way the text explains the Three Jewels. Next, the spiritual master is important:

> **Realizing that it is your preceptor who points out and introduces you to these Three Jewels, that he is endowed with the same virtues they have, and that he sustains you with kindliness, always attend and meditate upon him with unflagging faith.**

The preceptor or guru is important because the guru introduces you to the Buddha, Dharma, and Saṅgha. We don't have the good fortune to see the Buddha in real life, the actual Buddha, but we can hear the Buddha's teachings through the spiritual master. The Mahāyāna teachings do not explain that the master *is* Buddha, but that the spiritual master is *like* Buddha because he points you in the right direction and introduces you to the Three Jewels.

We are discussing the motivating factors—faith, compassion, and intention. The first one, faith, explains taking refuge in the Buddha, Dharma, Saṅgha, and your master or guru. The second motivating factor is compassion:

> **Since they are like yourself in having the nature of being endowed with the causes of pain and with a constant state of unsatisfactoriness, and like yourself, in wishing themselves to be free from unhappiness and its causes, you should unceasingly meditate great compassion for all living beings.**

All sentient beings indulge in negative deeds. Although their wish is to be free from the suffering that is caused by ignorance and negative emotions, they are constantly creating the causes of their continued suffering. And they experience very great suffering—the sufferings of birth, death, sickness, and old age, not just one time but again and again from beginningless time until now. All sentient beings, whether one is a believer or a nonbeliever, a Buddhist or a non-Buddhist, whatever ideas or philosophies one has, all of us wish to be free from suffering. We must generate great compassion for all sentient beings, knowing that they are just like ourselves in longing to be free from unhappiness and its causes. Cultivating this compassion is very important.

There are different kinds of compassion. There is compassion in reference to beings, compassion in reference to dharma, and compassion in reference to the objectless. These mean, respectively, the wish to liberate beings from actual suffering, the wish to liberate them from the causes of suffering, and the wish to liberate them from the very root of suffering.

Śrāvakas and pratyekabuddhas have compassion, but their compassion is not linked to actions. It is only mental compassion. The compassion of bodhisattvas is active and much more powerful and effective. In the beginning we said that compassion is important as a foundation. But it is also important as a motivating factor. In the Mahāyāna, the root of the teaching lies in compassion. It is important in the beginning, in the middle, and in the end.

The third motivating factor that is a prelude to the path is *intention*:

> **Recalling the benefits of virtue that you will need to attain highest enlightenment and to achieve others' good as well as your own purposes, strive wholeheartedly with genuine devotion to acquire it. In brief, since a mind endowed with faith, compassion, and intention is the precursor of all spiritual accomplishments, perform even the smallest virtue with these three present.**

Highest enlightenment, as I said, is called nonabiding nirvāṇa, which is that of a buddha possessing the three *kāyas*—the *dharmakāya*, saṃbhogakāya, and nirmāṇakāya—and having the inconceivable activities or qualities of a buddha. Recalling these qualities and benefits of virtue will strengthen your intention to acquire buddhahood. Whenever we practice, it is very important to have these three causes: faith, compassion, and intention. Every practice that we do must be done with the right causal motivations.

3. The Yoga of Meditation as the Core of the Path

Nāgārjuna has said that buddhas possess two bodies, the *rūpakāya*, or "form body," and the dharmakāya, or "body of ultimate reality." The means for accomplishing the rūpakāya is the practice of meditation with an object.

Our root text says:

> **Envision the body of the enlightened one either in front of you or as your own body, and visualize that your dwelling place is a buddha field wherein all beings are conquerors surrounded by bodhisattvas and disciples. Then worship yourself and others with oceans of offerings consisting of the enjoyment of the five sense objects.**

It says to envision, or meditate, and there are two ways of doing this. First, the Buddha can be visualized in front of you. This is, I suppose, the method taught for beginners or for those who do not have the courage to visualize themselves as the Buddha. If you are more familiar with the teachings and able to do the visualization, then you should visualize yourself in the form of Buddha. Visualize the image of the Buddha. The phrase "enlightened one" in the root verse is in Sanskrit *muni*, or "sage." Śrāvakas and pratyekabuddhas are inferior munis, and Buddha is the highest muni.

Visualize the Buddha surrounded by many disciples and bodhisattvas. "Disciples" means śrāvakas and pratyekabuddhas, and "bodhisattvas" means the sons of the Buddha. If you visualize yourself as the Buddha, then the śrāvakas, pratyekabuddhas, and bodhisattvas are all around you. This meditation is in the manner of Vajrayāna practices of visualizing yourself in the form of a deity.

There are many different quotations from many different texts that say that all sentient beings are Buddha. But of course, ordinary sentient beings and buddhas are totally different. Ordinary beings like us are helpless, without freedom or knowledge, and wherever the winds of karma blow we must go there. We must experience enormous amounts of suffering. Meanwhile, buddhas are totally free from karma and the defilements, and they have eliminated all forms of obscurations: the obscurations of the defilements and the obscurations of knowledge. They have gained omniscient wisdom and complete, ultimate realization. The difference is like that between sky and earth.

However, between the nature of our minds and the nature of the Buddhas's transcendental wisdom there is no difference; in the mind's own nature, there is no difference. This is why you can become a buddha if you make efforts. If you did not have this buddha nature, then no matter how hard you worked you could never become a buddha.

In order to accomplish the rūpakāya, or the physical form of the Buddha, we visualize ourselves as the Buddha or we visualize the Buddha in front of us, with golden color, with the thirty-two signs and the eighty qualities, and with many light rays issuing out.

If the Buddha were to come to us in real life, of course we would experience great devotion and not hesitate to make any kind of offering. But when we are visualizing the Buddha or standing before an image or a statue, even though we pay respects and we make offerings, we might not feel great faith in our minds and we might hesitate to make offerings. This is because of our defiled minds. In reality, there is no difference between seeing the actual Buddha in real life, seeing an image or a statue of the Buddha, and seeing the Buddha in our minds. Likewise, no matter where we go or where we are, the Buddha knows us. The things that we do, the devotion that we have, the offerings that we make, the faith we have—the Buddha knows each and every thing very clearly, as clearly as looking into one's own palm. Thus there is really no difference between these three.

In any case, you visualize the Buddha again and again in order to accumulate merit. Then, when you have very clear visualizations, you should think, "Where does this Buddha come from? Where it is residing? Where will it go?" When you examine the visualization in this way, you will realize that the Buddha has not come from anywhere, the Buddha does not remain anywhere, and the Buddha does not go anywhere. Through this practice, you can realize that all phenomena are similarly unarisen, unabiding, and unceasing, and you will develop wisdom as well as merit.

When you visualize the Buddha, you should also visualize the buddha field in which all beings are conquerors. The buddha field is made entirely of precious jewels, and it is smooth like your own palm. If you press on the ground, it goes down, and if you lift up, it goes up. Visualize all beings as either bodhisattvas or disciples—that is, śrāvakas and pratyekabuddhas.

Next, you should make offerings. These are five sense offerings: for the eyes, form; for the ears, sound; for the nose, smell; for the tongue, taste; and for the body, touch. If you have actual offering substances, then you should offer them. If not, produce mentally created offerings. The bodhisattva Samantabhadra made very special and inconceivable offerings, and you should think that you are offering like Samantabhadra by mentally creating inconceivably vast offerings. By doing this, you will gain great merit.

Your spiritual master should also be worshiped, as it says here:

> **Realize that your own virtuous preceptor and all the conquerors are truly equal and nondual in form, activity, and essential nature. At all times, you should envision him in front of you, or seated atop the crown of your head, or within the lotus of your heart, and pray to him or meditate upon him as nondual with yourself.**

The importance of the preceptor, or teacher, is emphasized from the vinaya all the way to the Vajrayāna teachings. This is because all of one's qualities have their source in the spiritual master. There are many qualifications or special characteristics that a guru must possess. As it is said by Lord Maitreya, the spiritual master should be gentle, knowledgeable, and so on. At minimum, the spiritual master should have three qualifications. First, he should be very disciplined; a master who does not have good discipline is not right. Second, he should have wisdom; he should be rich with knowledge of the Dharma. And third, he should have the compassion to teach disciples without any hesitation; he should have the patience, ability, and courage to teach.

Finding this kind of guru is very important, because meeting such a qualified guru is really the same as meeting the Buddha himself. The buddhas have great compassion; the Buddha loves every sentient being like a mother loves her only child. However, due to lack of merit and bad fortune, we are not in a circumstance to see the Buddha in our lifetime. We cannot hear the Buddha speak, and we cannot receive the Buddha's blessings directly. Through the medium of the guru, however, we receive both the teachings and the blessings of the Buddha. The guru is like an instrument that brings us the energy of the sun. The sun is always shining brightly in the sky, but without proper instruments we cannot utilize its energy. Similarly, without the guru one cannot receive the blessings of the Buddha.

Even though he appears in ordinary human form, you should think that your guru is physically, verbally, and mentally the same as the Buddha, and always have great devotion. Practice visualizing the guru in front of you, or on the crown of your head, or in the lotus of your heart. In the higher guru yogas, it says that during the day you should visualize the guru at the crown of your head, and at night you should visualize him in the lotus of your heart. In this way you can receive his blessings at all times, and you will experience protection from all forms of obstacles.

These are practices of the kind we call *meditation with an object*. Through these meditations, you will receive all the good qualities and benefits of saṃsāra as well as nirvāṇa. The first practice is to visualize the Buddha surrounded by bodhisattvas and then make offerings. In the next practice, guru yoga, it says that we should have devotion, but it does not say that we should make offerings—but actually it is the same for both. As you meditate on the image of the Buddha, you should have devotion and you should make offerings, and in the guru yoga, you should have devotion and you should also make offerings.

In this way, we will accumulate the merit heap. To accomplish buddhahood, you need heaps of both merit and wisdom, just as a bird flies in the sky with two wings. By visualizing the buddhas and bodhisattvas, by making offerings and generating devotion, you will accumulate merit. Eventually, when you attain buddhahood, you will gain the physical form of a buddha with the thirty-two signs and the eighty qualities—the golden color and so on—and you will also gain the buddha fields. All the visible qualities of buddhahood are gained through the accumulation of the merit heap.

The other attainment is the dharmakāya, and in order to accomplish it we practice *objectless meditation*. The dharmakāya is accomplished through the accumulation of transcendental wisdom, and in order to attain this, one must practice objectless meditation. It says here:

> **Of virtue, nonvirtue, pleasure, pain, and all the phenomena of saṃsāra and nirvāṇa, mind is the substratum.**

The word *virtue* in this case is, I believe, what is called *kuśala* in Sanskrit. *Ku* means "bad," and *sala* means "to give up" or "to abstain." By *virtue* is meant abstinence from actions like killing and stealing. *Saṃsāra* means conceptual thought or the stream of conceptual thought. And *nirvāṇa* means without conceptual thought.

This verse means that everything—all the things that we see, all pain and all pleasure—are the mind. It is the mind that does wrong things, and it is the mind that does right things. It is the mind that experiences happiness, and it is the mind that experiences suffering. It is the mind that falls into the lower realms, and it is the mind that is born into the higher realms. It is the mind that attains liberation and enlightenment. For everything, the root lies in the mind.

When the mind abstains from wrongdoing, there is virtue. When the mind does not abstain from wrongdoing, there is sin. If you realize the nature of mind, that is nirvāṇa. If you do not realize the nature of mind, that is saṃsāra. From beginningless time until now, we have not been able to realize the nature of mind, no matter how hard we have tried, and this is why we are caught up in saṃsāra, over and over again. So what we must do is begin to examine this mind.

> **If you were to examine that mind thoroughly from every angle, you would realize that it has neither color nor shape, nor is it single or manifold. It therefore has no nature; therefore it is not arisen, neither does it remain nor cease. It is devoid of both**

center and periphery and is thus away from all extremes. It has just the nature of space.

If you begin to examine the mind through study, contemplation, and meditation, you will not find it. In the same way that you cannot locate space, you cannot find the mind. It has no inherent existence. If it had inherent existence, then it would have to be in some form. If it had form, it would also have color, shape, or size. But mind has no color, shape, or size.

If mind had inherent existence, it would have to be either one or many. But with mind you cannot find one or many. Mind has no root, no place, no base, no sign, no color, no shape, and it is beyond perception. Therefore it is never arising, never born, and never ceasing.

Anything that arises must arise from a cause. But when we analyze causality, we see that the cause and the result occur in different times. The cause is in one moment and the result is in another moment, and they do not meet. If they exist simultaneously, then which one causes the other? If there is no cause, then how can anything arise? If we say that they arise together, then there cannot be a distinction made between one as cause and the other as result. If it could arise without any cause, then it would have to have always been at all times.

Therefore the mind is never arising. Because it is never arising, it is never residing. Something that is never residing can never cease. Mind has no center and no edges, and it is away from both extremes of existence and nonexistence.

Ordinary people do not ever bother to wonder about the nature of reality. More intelligent people ask themselves, "Why we are here? What is the nature of things?" and they wonder if what we ordinarily see differs from the true nature of reality. People who have jaundice might see the moon as yellow, but that is not the reality of things. For them, of course, it is very clear that the moon is yellow, but they see it that way because of their illness. The things that we see—houses, temples, trees, mountains, water, so many different things—appear to us in the same way that the yellow moon appears for those with jaundice. Our defilements and our illusions create the appearance of these samsaric things. But reality is something different.

Some thoughtful people try to find out what reality is. After careful examination, people have found many different answers. Non-Buddhist schools have many different answers, and within Buddhism, too, there are many different philosophical schools. The ultimate or the primary answer that the Buddha taught is called "the perfection of wisdom." Later on, it was further expounded by Nāgārjuna. The Buddha gave a prophecy that after his mahāparinirvāṇa a bhikṣu named Nāga would come who would be able to explain the truth. Just as the Buddha prophesied, Nāgārjuna explained the philosophy of the Middle Way school.

Nāgārjuna explained all phenomena in two ways: the *relative* truth and the *absolute* truth. Relative truth takes reality to be as it appears in an unexamined way. Relatively speaking, there is a self, there are beings, there is experience, and so on. After examining this with very sharp reasoning, he found that—at the absolute level—it is impossible to say conclusively that reality is like this or like that. This is his fundamental difference from all other schools. Ultimate reality is beyond explanation, beyond words, beyond perception, beyond speech. It is away from all extremes—the extremes of existing, nonexisting, both existing and nonexisting, and neither existing nor nonexisting—and it is devoid of arising, residing, and ceasing.

But one might wonder, if even the mind is not real, if it is never found, then what is this mind that investigates?

> **Even so, cognition is not stopped. Hence mind has the nature of nondual cognition and emptiness.**

"Cognition" is awareness. Of course, when you examine the mind, you cannot locate it anywhere. Everything is created by the mind, but when you search for the mind you cannot find it. Nevertheless, you cannot say that there is no mind. If it were true that there is no mind at all, then you would be just a lifeless body or entirely without consciousness. But we are awake, we are alive, and we have this very vivid awareness and clarity that is devoid of reality.

It is not that the mind *is* emptiness. *Emptiness* does not mean empty like an empty house without things in it. It is not like this. Rather, when you try to search for the mind, you cannot find it, but at the same time there is something that we all can feel, which is awareness. Awareness and emptiness are inseparable, just like fire and the heat of fire. Emptiness is not separate from clarity or awareness, and clarity is not separate from emptiness. The two are inseparable. One should realize in this way.

As one's own mind is, so too is the nature of all beings' minds.

Every other being's mind is the same in being the nonduality of emptiness and awareness.

Understand thoroughly that all phenomena are nondual appearance and emptiness, and place your mind in meditation without grasping.

All phenomena including the mind are the nonduality of appearance and emptiness. We may see many things, but when we investigate we cannot find anything except the nonduality of appearance and emptiness. One cannot say that things do not exist. They are visible to our consciousness. We see them. But at the same time, when you examine closely and you try to find them, you cannot. There is only the complete nonduality of appearance and emptiness.

According to the *Heart Sūtra*, "Form is emptiness, emptiness form. Form is not other than emptiness, emptiness is not other than form." This is to say that appearance and emptiness are completely nondual. One should realize all of one's own mind as well as all phenomena to be thus.

Through meditating nondually on the two objects [one's preceptor and the enlightened one] and objectlessness [emptiness], you will attain a superior meditative state of tranquil concentration [śamatha] that cannot be disturbed by thoughts.

As we have explained, the text presents two kinds of meditation: meditation with an object and meditation without an object. Meditation with an object has two types: visualizing the guru and visualizing the Buddha. Altogether, this makes three meditations. One accumulates merit through the meditations practiced with an object, and one accumulates wisdom through the practice of meditation without an object.

By performing these meditations, you will achieve a state of completely tranquil concentration. At the moment, our minds are very busy so that even though we may try to sit and see into the nature of mind, we remain unable to accomplish this. In the beginning, especially, so many thoughts arise that you might become discouraged at your inability to meditate. But this stream of thoughts is actually present all the time. Normally we are so busy that we do not see this, and only when we try to sit in meditation do we realize that so many thoughts are arising. Recognizing this is actually a sign that you are meditating properly, so you should certainly not be discouraged. In the beginning, one cannot meditate for long periods of time, and it is best to practice for short periods—but to do many sessions. This way eventually you will be able to remain in single-pointed concentration in a very clear way. This provides the base for actual meditation and is very good.

Because the meditations that we do are also thoughts, you may wonder how actual meditation can arise from them. It is said that in ancient times, in order to make fire, people rubbed two sticks of wood together. Fire and wood are different. Yet by rubbing two pieces of wood together one can create fire, and the fire can completely burn away the wood that produced it. Similarly, in meditation with an object there are thoughts, but eventually objectless meditation will arise from this. This is the actual meditation, and with objectless meditation you can realize the ultimate truth.

Of course, to realize the ultimate truth you must make great efforts, and you need not only meditation but also merit. Through meditation with an object you can accumulate merit, and through meditation without an object you can create wisdom. Like the bird that flies in the sky with two wings, with the merit heap and with the wisdom heap one will be able to accomplish the result.

4. Subsequent Efforts and Methods for Deepening the Virtues of the Path

Joyfully remembering that every act of virtue or nonvirtue increases the strength of one's virtuous or nonvirtuous inclinations always bring virtues to mind and strengthens them.

Virtuous deeds are not to be wasted. Rejoicing in them will increase their strength, and we should therefore remember virtues again and again. Virtuous deeds done by others will be a cause for us to earn great merit if we rejoice in them and if we support them without any jealousy or competitive thoughts. One should also rejoice in one's own virtues, in virtuous things that one may have done such as making offerings or helping other beings, and so on. One should think, "I have done something that is helpful, that is meritorious." This increases the strength of the virtuous deeds so that one will always be earning more and more merit.

The nonvirtuous deeds that we have done should be regretted. Learning to regret nonvirtuous deeds is a very effective practice. If you commit a nonvirtuous deed and feel that what you did was right, if you think, "I have done something good; what I have done is good," then it becomes stronger in your mind, and it will bring about more severe consequences. Therefore you should always generate strong regret for whatever nonvirtuous deeds you have done; think, "I made a serious mistake, harmful to myself and others, and I should not have done that thing. It was a great mistake."

Also, you should tell your nonvirtuous deeds to others, and you should keep your virtuous deeds private. You should not show them off but rejoice in them privately, thinking, "I have done something very good, and it will earn merit and it will benefit beings." If you have done nonvirtuous deeds, then you should not keep them private. You should say that you have made a big mistake. This will reduce the strength of the nonvirtue in your mind, and it will reduce the severity of the consequences.

Especially should you recollect and analyze the support, form, and experience of your meditation whenever you have medi-

> **tated upon an object. Examining further the interdependent origination of their causes and conditions, however many they may be, you will attain meditative insight [vidarśanā] through realizing the true state of their suchness—that is, through realizing that no support, form, or experience whatsoever exists.**

Whenever you perform virtuous deeds, you should recollect them, but in particular, when you have done meditation with an object, with an image of the Buddha, then you should recollect the meditation and examine the object and examine the mind and analyze the causes and conditions of each. When you examine the meditation in this way, you will realize the interdependently originated nature of phenomena—that it is all connected, and that without this cause and that condition, this or that experience will not arise.

For example, when there is a clear sky, a bright moon, and a pot of clear water, the reflection of the moon will appear on the water. Whatever the number of pots, each one will have one reflection of the moon. For this reflection to appear, you need many things: a clear sky, a bright moon, clear water, the pot, and so on. There are many causes and conditions necessary for the image to occur.

A modern example is the television. In order for the picture to appear on the screen, you need many things to come together in a precise way: wiring and electricity, an antenna, and so on. If even a tiny wire is missing then the picture will not appear. Similarly, the life that we experience, the practice that we do—everything is interdependently originated. Everything originates in dependence on other things, and without the right causes and conditions things will not appear. If things had inherent existence, then they would not depend upon causes and conditions but would appear completely independently of any other thing. But because everything depends upon causes and conditions, it shows that there is no possible inherent existence.

If, on the basis of good concentration or śamatha, one practices examination in this way, then one will acquire insight wisdom—one will be able to realize ultimate truth.

Following the performance of virtues, you should gather together all the merits acquired through that [meditation and the like] and fully dedicate them to the attainment of perfect enlightenment by yourself and all these countless beings.

Dedication is very important. If you do not dedicate merit, then whatever virtuous deeds that you have done can be spoiled by the arising of a strong opposite emotion such as anger. It is important that any virtuous deed that you do be dedicated before it is wasted or affected by any negative thing.

The way to practice dedication is very specific. Combine together whatever virtuous deeds that you have done in the past, whatever virtuous deeds that you are doing now, and whatever virtuous deeds that you will do in the future, and then dedicate all of them together.

The superior way to dedicate merit is by realizing that all three realms—"three realms" here means the object of merit, the being creating merit, and the action of creating merit—are in reality devoid of arising, remaining, and cessation. It is difficult for ordinary beings to perceive or realize emptiness, or the wisdom of *śūnyatā*, but thinking that these three realms are devoid of arising, remaining, and cessation is the best way to dedicate one's merit.

The mediocre way to dedicate merit is to realize that whatever merit we have acquired has no inherent existence and is like a magical show or a dream. It's easy to know that dreams are not real when we are awake, but while we're dreaming they are as real as this life. During dreams, you feel happiness, sadness, fear, or anxiety. All kinds of experiences can arise. Similarly, the life we are going through now is like a dream; it is not real. It is like a magical show or an illusion. So you should dedicate merit with this thought.

The inferior way to dedicate merit is just to think that you will dedicate merit like the great bodhisattvas Mañjuśrī and Avalokiteśvara, and so on, do. Not knowing how to dedicate properly, just think that you dedicate your own merit in the same way that they dedicated merit.

While the virtuous deed and the merit acquired from it are still fresh and unaffected by any strong opposite factor, you should dedicate it to the attainment of full enlightenment for the sake of all sentient beings. When you dedicate merit in this way, it will not be affected by strong opposite emotions such as anger. Moreover, it will cause the merit to increase all the time, like earning interest.

> **Even though transferable merit may not have been acquired at the time you offer prayers, your wishes nonetheless will be fulfilled if you pray for a great purpose to be achieved, for mind alone is chief.**

This is the power of prayer or aspiration. It is even possible to dedicate future merit, and this will be effective because everything is mind. Mind alone is most important.

> **Every virtue that is adorned by this kind of recollection, dedication, and noble prayer will increase unceasingly and eventually become the cause of great good for oneself and others.**

Whenever we do a virtuous deed, we should have good motivation; we should rejoice in it; and we should dedicate the merit at the end. In this way, even if it is something small, it will always increase and will not be wasted.

Whatever nonvirtuous deed that we have committed should be regretted again and again. If you feel guilty, it will decrease the strength of the nonvirtue.

With these practices, your merit is increasing and your nonvirtuous deeds are decreasing, and with that, you can accomplish the great purpose.

5. Infusion of All the Paths and Elements of the Dharma

Everything that is experienced and all other conditioned things [*saṃskṛtadharma*]—the five aggregates, senses, sense objects, and sense consciousnesses—are devoid of any nature of their own because they all depend upon causes and conditions.

At the relative level, we should see everything as an illusion or as a magic show.

Everything depends upon causes and conditions, and everything therefore lacks inherent nature, as demonstrated in the example of the reflection of the moon on water. Similarly, everything and every practice that we do is devoid of self-nature, devoid of inherent existence, but at the same time appears. For this reason, it is to be understood as like an illusion or a magic show.

> **Therefore you should know that these external objects, appearing in various forms to, and experienced by, mind, which is stained by mental impressions, are not real. They are like magic shows that appear due to a variety of causes. They are also like dreams that occur during sleep.**

Even though they are not real, objects appear due to our propensities and so on. People say that "seeing is believing," but, of course, we see many things that are not real: dreams, for example, or magic shows. In a magic show, through special substances and mantras, a magician can make many things appear, but it is easy to realize that they are not real. One should see all phenomena as like a dream or like a magic show.

> **The so-called unconditioned *dharmas* [*asaṃskṛtadharma*] are simply ascriptions. A person would have to be mad to wish to propose meaningless names for them, or to indulge in thoughts about them and thereby accept them as conditioned dharmas.**

Space, for example, is not created through causes and conditions. It is just thought, and it is not real. When compounded things are understood to be not real, then such uncompounded things as this are also obviously not real.

> **Never scorn the connection between deeds and their results, for the teachings on the interdependent origination of cause and**

result as it operates in the sphere of relative truth are not deceptive. You will experience the ripening results of your actions.

As I have already said, Nāgārjuna explained all phenomena by means of the two truths, the relative truth and the absolute, or ultimate, truth. Until one realizes ultimate truth, one has to go through relative truth and one must be very careful, following the law of karma. Everything is dependent origination, and whatever deeds that we do produce results. Although, in reality, there is no cause and result—although, in reality, there is nothing to be abandoned and nothing to take—until we realize this truth, each and every entity and phenomenon at the relative level has it own causes and conditions, and will never fail to produce results. Even very small negative deeds will produce negative results. And even very small virtuous deeds will produce positive results. Until one realizes the ultimate truth, it is important that one follows the law of karma.

Some people say that everything is impermanent, everything is śūnyatā, and in śūnyatā whatever you do—good or bad, virtuous or nonvirtuous—makes no difference. However, until you realize the ultimate truth, you must be very careful. As the text says, "You will experience the ripening result of your actions."

There are eternalists in whose view the substantiality of phenomena is accepted. However, no object whatsoever exists that is devoid of direction [dimension] and time [consciousness]. If you were to analyze the forms of direction and space, you could not possibly find a single entity that is not reducible to its component parts. And if a single entity does not exist, how could many appear? As there is no existence other than these, the conceptualization of existence is an inferior one.

There are two different schools of philosophy that must be rejected. They represent the two extreme views called *eternalism* and *nihilism*, respectively. The first, eternalism, accepts the substantial existence of phenomena. How is this wrong view refuted? An entity must be either a "thing" or consciousness. If it is a thing, then it must have direction or dimension. Even the smallest thing, said to be irreducible, also must have direction. If you keep dividing in this way, then you cannot find anything. Time is similarly divisible. Anything that has dimension or is divisible has for that reason constituent parts of which it is compounded. And when you cannot find a single phenomenon anywhere, how can you find many? Everything arises interdependently.

> **Just as there is no length without shortness, how could a nature of nonexistence be apprehended when even a nature of existence is not obtained?**

The second school, nihilism, claims that nothing exists. Many different schools lean to the existence side and many lean to the nonexistence side. But if you adhere to any of these extreme views, then there will be no way to accomplish realization. Ultimate truth is away from all existence and nonexistence.

> **Know, intelligent one, that the real also does not consist of both existence and nonexistence because this possibility has been removed by the rejection of each individually; nor does it consist of being neither of these two, because there is no logical proof for this possibility, and, in any case, there is no possible bothness to which this could be an alternative.**

> **But if we were to conclude that mind alone is real since it is formless and thus has no directions, we would have to admit that it also becomes plural and false if subject and object are identical [the latter being manifold].**

This is because the subject, or mind, has to hold many different objects, so it could not be just one.

> **If, however, subject and object are different from one another, how then do objects become objectified and mind subjectified? If the two arise dually, in what way [for example, simultaneously**

or otherwise] do they appear? Finally, what kind of liberation is achieved merely by rejecting illusory external appearances?

Subject and object depend upon each other. If there are no objects, no phenomena or things, if outer or external things are not real, then in what way could a subject arise? They depend upon each other, so that if one does not exist, the other cannot possibly exist.

Since the object is not established as real by nature, the subject, too, is not established as real. The claim that there exists somehow a pure consciousness apart from these two is as extremely wrong as the Sāṃkhya philosophers' notion of a self [*puruṣa*] distinct from the transformations of primal nature [*prakṛti*].

Be free from supports, knowing that all phenomena from the first are unarisen, natureless, away from extremes, and like space.

Marvelous and much more wondrous than any wonder is this knowledge that does not relinquish the emptiness of all dharmas nor stop the process of interdependent origination!

All appearance that we see—forms, sounds, and so on—are interdependently originated. Due to many causes and conditions, this or that appears, and this process never ceases. It goes on and on. At the same time, it is all emptiness. Saying that everything arises due to interdependent origination also means that everything is emptiness. If phenomena were truly real, they would not arise dependently. If something depends on other things, then it shows that it is not inherently real. It has no inherent existence.

As long as you think of appearance and emptiness as separate, then this is not the ultimate view. The ultimate view is that appearance and emptiness are not unbalanced; they are completely balanced together, and they are inseparable. Appearance and emptiness are inseparable. Sound and emptiness are inseparable. Awareness and emptiness are inseparable. It says here:

Realize that objects are the nonduality of appearance and emptiness, that mind is the nonduality of knowledge and emptiness, and that the path to liberation is the nonduality of method and wisdom.

Finally, act [in accord with this insight].

The stages of cause, path, and result should be understood thus: the interdependent origination of the relative sphere is like illusion; in the ultimate, the nature of dharmas is emptiness; finally, both are nondual without differentiation.

The cause or base is the nonduality of the two truths, the relative truth and the absolute truth. The path is the nonduality of method and wisdom. And the result is the nonduality of the rūpakāya and the dharmakāya. Thus we have all three: the cause, the path, and the result.

Thus if the foundation [morality], preparation [reflection], meditation, conclusion [dedication of merit and recollection], and the process of practice taken as a whole is each multiplied by three [in correspondence to the three stages of cause, path, and result], all the paths of virtue are gathered together in fifteen factors.

In the beginning, we said that in order to practice you need the following five things: the base; the motivating factors; meditation; the factors for increasing; and finally the infusion, the seal. If we apply these five things three times—for base, path, and result—it makes fifteen factors. This is the correct way to practice. Having practiced, then, what kind of result will be gained?

Whoever strives to perfect these factors in each performance of virtue enjoys the happiness of fortunate states and accumu-

lates oceans of the two collections of merit and transcendent wisdom.

"Fortunate states" means higher rebirth: birth in the human realm, the demigod realm, or the god realm. Also, by continuing to perfect these factors, one accumulates the two collections. This verse says that you will gain the result of the path of accumulation.

The path of accumulation is the first of the five paths mentioned earlier: the path of accumulation, the path of application, the path of seeing, the path of meditation, and the path of no-more-learning. The path of accumulation and the path of application are called the two worldly paths, meaning they are still at the worldly level. The path of accumulation is primarily the accumulation of merits.

Through the clarity of his meditation, he becomes joined with the Āryan path and increases in transcendent wisdom as a result of his meditation and noble conduct. Then, attaining the goal [of buddhahood] through coursing along the final stages of the path, he puts an end to all thought constructions by realizing the nature of mind to be pure from the very beginning. His mind becomes one flavor with the dharmadhātu and is transformed into the svabhāvakāya, which is the transcendent wisdom of dharmadhātu and the knowledge of the perfection of renunciation.

The "Āryan path" is the path of application, the second of the five paths. It joins the worldly level to the beyond-worldly level. You enter the path of seeing, the third path, from the path of application at the time when you first see ultimate reality. This is also the first *bhūmi*, the first of the ten stages on the path to enlightenment.

The difference between the first bhūmi and ultimate enlightenment is like the difference between the new moon and the full moon. It is the same moon. Then, as you increase in wisdom, you will enter the path of meditation, the fourth path, which, according to the Pāramitāyāna, has nine stages. On each stage, you increase your wisdom, like the moon increases from the first moon onward. And then, finally, you will reach the full moon, which is buddhahood.

> **For him, the dharmas of worldly existence become transformed through the practice of the path so that his body becomes the body of an enlightened one adorned by 112 marks and signs of perfection; his voice becomes the voice of a buddha endowed with sixty tones; his mind is transformed into transcendent wisdom and is also endowed with omniscience. Passions are transformed into the boundless virtues of the conqueror and constitute the saṃbhogakāya. His deeds are transformed into the task accomplishing wisdom and the countless kinds of enlightened activity that form the nirmāṇakāya.**

The thirty-two signs and the eighty qualities make up the 112 "marks and signs of perfection." The Buddha has five wisdoms: the wisdom of the dharmadhātu, mirror-like wisdom, the wisdom of equality, the wisdom of discrimination, and the wisdom of accomplishment. The wisdom of the dharmadhātu is the same thing as the dharmakāya. It is actually the nature of all things.

As I said before, there is no difference between the nature of our minds and the Buddha's nature of transcendental wisdom, which is the dharmakāya. The dharmakāya is not something new to be gained. It is what we already have. At the present moment, we possess the dharmakāya because the nature of our minds is naturally pure. Mind in its nature is never stained with obscurations, although at the moment we are unable to recognize it. The moment that the obscurations are cleared, you will see the nature of your mind: it is the dharmakāya.

What you will gain after clearing the obscurations is the thiry-two signs and eighty qualities of a buddha's form. You will have a body of gold, a voice with the sixty melodies of Dharma, and a mind with omniscient wisdom comprising mirror-like wisdom, the wisdom of discrimination, the wisdom of equality, and so on. The wisdom of accomplishment is the nirmāṇakāya. The physical qualities together with the other wisdoms are the saṃbhogakāya. In this way, buddhahood, with the three kāyas and the five transcendental wisdoms, will be accomplished.

> **These five wisdoms constitute the perfect realization of the enlightened one, and, inasmuch as he is also endowed with spiritual power, they are unending and uninterrupted. May you also, O emperor, become like him!**

The Buddha's activities never cease; they continue as long as space remains.

The remaining verses comprise a conclusion and dedication. These are things that are mentioned for the sake of the emperor. So with this, we conclude the teaching.

1. Central image: Sachen Kunga Nyingpo; upper left: Sönam Tsemo; upper right: Jetsun Drakpa Gyaltsen; lower left: Sakya Paṇḍita; lower right: Chögyal Phagpa; bottom left: Ngorchen Kunga Sangpo; bottom right: Tsarchen Losal Gyatso.

2. Drogön Chögyal Phagpa receiving teachings from his teacher, Sakya Paṇḍita.

3. Drogön Chögyal Phagpa teaching at the Mongol court.

4. Photo of His Holiness Kyabgon Gongma Trichen Rinpoche.

Part Three

A Garland of Jewels

4. Root Verses of *A Garland of Jewels*

Drogön Chögyal Phagpa

Homage Verses

Prostrations to all buddhas and bodhisattvas.

Prostrations to the Buddha, who is like Mount Sumeru and whose magnificent body is born from an ocean of merit and wisdom, adorned with unfathomable qualities.

Born in the land of oceans of merit; splendid in race, wealth, and physical appearance; competently ruling country and subjects: may you have victory, glorious jewel-like prince.

I, Phagpa, possess a base of pure moral conduct and uphold great teachings like an ocean abounds with precious jewels. From my ocean-mind the words of this teaching arise like a garland of jewels illuminating every direction with its radiance, an ornament beautifying both self and others. This is offered with a virtuous mind.

What is the point of making material gifts to one with such immense wealth? Instead, I offer this gift of Dharma to illuminate, like moonlight at midnight opens the kunda flower.

I

Possessing a wealth of worldly riches but lacking the riches of Dharma is like enjoying delicious food that is mixed with poison and only begets suffering.

Conversely, possessing the riches of Dharma but lacking worldly wealth is like an encrusted gem that cannot serve the purpose of others.

However, by possessing both types of wealth, the purposes of both self and others can be accomplished, like a well-cut jewel that beautifies both self and others.

Therefore, in order to render fruitful the two glories with which you are endowed, I have carefully considered these words.

If even the brilliance of the sun, the depth of the ocean, and the loftiness of Mount Sumeru will disappear at the end of time, what need to mention the wealth of sentient beings?

Realizing this, do not be arrogant because of your immense wealth. Always rely on mindfulness in order to increase the gloriousness of your glory.

Having tasted suffering, develop renunciation. Even happiness is subject to change. Everything conditioned arises out of a cause. Perceiving that this cause is the cause of suffering, do not let your mind be defiled. Bend your mind to become the condition for the accumulation of merit through experiencing the afflictions of oneself and others.

It is through the confluence of merit and prayer that your body, directly and indirectly, came into being from your father's and mother's lineage. Therefore reflect on their kindness. By cultivating a virtuous way of life, your hereditary lineage will flow like a river, and, having concern for your subjects, your wishes will be fulfilled.

Having depended totally on the Buddha's glory, make known his kindness, venerating him always like a jewel on your crown. Just as he, like a jewel, bestows upon you fulfillment of each and every need, similarly you will also be worthy of others' veneration.

Among the various types of people, be considerate of, respect, and care for the elderly among your subjects, the truthful among speakers, the authentic tradition among traditions, the altruistic among ascetics, the wealth of wisdom among the various types of wealth, the wise among the respected, the destitute among the inferior, the sick among the destitute, the one who follows you among your spouses, the one who will carry on your lineage among sons, the one who never deceives you among relatives, the one who benefits you among friends, the one who obeys your orders among attendants, the one who repays your kindness among those whom you have benefited, the one able to remain patient among those whom you may have harmed, the one who suddenly appears among all. Through this, others will be inspired and also engage in moral conduct.

Fishermen, butchers, and the like who harm others will never accomplish their own purpose. What need to mention their accomplishing the purpose of others?

The inferior, middling, and superior levels of the disciples, bodhisattvas, and victors are determined by the extent of their benefit to others. Although this is not obvious, you can identify a small, medium, or great lord because he will be benefiting others in a small, medium, or great way.

Therefore if you have loving-kindness toward all sentient beings, what need to mention the obligation to have loving-kindness toward those who depend upon you?

Know that all the lives that depend upon you are equal. It is not the way of the Dharma to satisfy a few people by killing others.

Sensually delightful activities, free of defilements, gratify many. Though you may indulge at appropriate times to be rid of boredom, under careful reflection, know that it creates a cause of suffering to indulge unwisely in temporary pleasures by harming others. Realizing this, abandon such actions.

One constantly makes mistakes oneself yet does not tolerate the faults of others. There is no contradiction greater than to kill the innocent for this.

One will become an inspiration by showing compassion, be worshiped by caring for others, and be praised by speaking pleasantly. Such is the reality of phenomena.

Shouldn't the practices of loving-kindness and accomplishing others' benefit also be engaged by those striving only for this worldly life, no need to mention for the sake of enlightenment?

Realizing this, practice loving-kindness and the benefit of others. This will accomplish one's own and others' purpose in this and the next life.

Hardship is necessary to increase one's lifespan, wealth, and Dharma practice. If any of these are not going well, overcome the difficulty through persistence.

Understand what scholars have said: wealth protects the retinue, the retinue protects the body, the body protects life, and all of them protect the Dharma.

Even though at times, certain religious or worldly pursuits may be unsuccessful, do not be discouraged. Look at the actions of businessmen and farmers.

It is extremely difficult to accomplish an important task all at once, but even the hardest can be accomplished by undertaking it gradually, like the case of an ant and its nest.

Many opposing factors arise when undertaking a substantial task, and even a single arrow alone is enough to kill.

Beneficial actions, like the atoms of an ocean, are never too plentiful; wouldn't the king of a larger kingdom be correspondingly greater?

Possessing skillful means, even harmful beings can be won over, like a hook that tames a wild elephant and renders it serviceable to the world.

Though worldly beings say enemies should be pacified through violent means, peaceful means can pacify—it's just like fire to fire and water to water.

Although a single harmful being may be subdued by violent means, *one* will only increase to many. This is similar to what happens to the pebbles of the riverbank when some are removed.

If through skillful means you can multiply those in your favor, you will become more stable, just as a house built upon a solid mountain is more stable.

Overcoming opposition in this manner, rule those under your power religiously because Dharma brings happiness to the world.

Rule the country and subjects kind-heartedly, speak pleasantly, confer titles accordingly, and fulfill material needs generously.

By ruling in this way, your wealth will increase like rain that falls upon all the guests gathered at a party. Does not the farmer reap what he has sown in his field?

Although all the subjects are equal, you should punish those who are not lawful and reward those who are. This is like an illness and the strength of the body.

Punishments should be given only in order to rehabilitate: scolding, beating, confiscating, and condemning. The death sentence should never be handed down. The wise wash dirty clothes and wear them again. Who would think it wise to dispose of them by burning?

Give recognition according to actions, and take it away if it is not appropriate. Reflect on the different ways of presenting food to babies, children, and adults.

A person without any good qualities and a person without any faults do not exist in this world. Examining what is frequent and what is infrequent, accept a fire torch even though it is smoky, abandon poison even though it is tasty, and use a horse cart while on the ground and a boat while in the water.

Understand that there are four kinds of wealth: wealth that is like an enemy, wealth that is like one's relative, purposeless wealth, and actual wealth.

First acquired and accumulated, then increased and protected, finally becoming harmful through quarreling and infighting—this is wealth that is like an enemy.

Wealth that is honestly obtained, effortlessly accumulated, and given with a virtuous mind: such wealth that creates benefit is wealth that is like one's relatives.

Wealth obtained through means that are neither good nor devious, wealth that is neither given nor used but is only hoarded all the time and then dissipated, such wealth is wealth without any purpose.

Obtained at the beginning either with little or much difficulty, the wealth that is utilized by oneself and for others for temporary comfort, such is the actual wealth.

Among these, always abandon the first and the third. Always use the second, and use the fourth as wished.

Indulging without any contentment begets suffering. Understand how decline of strength and indigestion arise.

Alcohol causes one to be despised by others, ruins one's body, weakens one's intelligence, ruins purpose, and separates one from the spiritual path. Therefore always look upon alcohol as a poison.

Moreover, attachment to sensual objects depletes the merits accumulated and always undermines one's capacity. Therefore always rely on contentment.

Even when conducting an activity, it is wise to carry out only after examination, and foolish to examine after performed. This is found in the scriptures of the noble beings. Carry out every action only after examination and discussion, and you will fulfill all your goals. Even if it turns out otherwise, there will be no regrets.

In short, be neither arrogant when wealthy nor downcast when impoverished. Repay kindnesses to those who serve you well. Venerate those worthy of veneration, and protect the weak. Exercise control over other territories and rule your own lands and subjects according to the Dharma. Utilize wealth with alertness and accomplish activities in a noble way.

II

By doing like this, one will be glorious and prosperous in this world. Through this, tread the path of Dharma in order to gain the happiness of worldly life.

There are many teachers, and each one guides along a different path. Even though there is only one teacher who has eliminated all faults and the causes of those faults and who has perfected all good qualities and is supreme, no one would say, "I have little knowledge" or "I am full of faults." Discern each teacher's qualities from his character and teaching.

A teaching that is free from any stains of spoken or written mistake, that is completely substantiated by the two valid cognitions, that completely abandons contradictions and inconsistencies, and that brings certain benefit and happiness belongs to a noble tradition. A master who discovers on his own such a noble tradition is supreme among masters, and those who follow his teaching also become noble.

Followers who practice with pure faith in the Buddha, the bodhisattvas, the Dharma, and disciples are noble. Therefore you, too, realizing the good qualities of the Buddha, the Dharma, and the Saṅgha, in order to be rescued from fear, should faithfully take the teacher, the path, and the companions as the ultimate refuge as long as you live.

This is the great foundation of all good qualities capable of clearing away all faults. Thus entering the door of Dharma dependent upon the supreme refuge, always act according to the Dharma, whose foundation is moral conduct.

Be wholesome by keeping the eight-limbed vows of a lay practitioner for a day and night. The Buddha has said that one will be born as a heavenly being of the desire realm by practicing ethical discipline.

Abide by the precepts of individual liberation in order to abandon attachment, which causes future rebirth, to abandon objects of distraction, and to maintain pure moral conduct.

If you are not able to uphold all the precepts, hold any according to your ability. Upholding even a single precept enhances your practice of moral conduct. When it becomes familiar, virtue will naturally increase without difficulty.

To become learned in all knowledge and to become liberated, incline your mind to listen; extensively study and discuss various types of logical reasoning and traditions. Those who are learned in all fields of knowledge, particularly possessing the ability to discriminate well, never make the mistakes of accepting what is wrong and rejecting what is right.

Particularly listen to teachings without becoming satiated by extensive Dharma. Dharma is the essence of knowledge and the means to greater wisdom and merit. With a doubting mind it is difficult to fulfill one's own purpose. Similarly, if you listen but don't understand the meaning, it is difficult to fulfill one's aim. Therefore analyze what you learn with valid reasoning and you will be able to ascertain the meaning clearly, as your eyes can see objects clearly.

Thus through dedication in listening to teachings and analyzing them, little by little your wisdom will increase, like a honeycomb is built by honeybees.

These are the skillful means for mastering the teachings. Just as grain is harvested through effort, so realization is attained through study.

By ascertaining the suffering of saṃsāra and its causes, which are karma and negative emotions, one increases virtuous actions.

By remaining in meditation analyzing the repulsiveness of the body, loving-kindness, interdependent origination, categories of elements, mindfulness of inhalation and exhalation of breath, and objective and subjective phenomena, one will attain the happiness of the higher realms.

Then traverse the worldly paths of accumulation and application, and the supramundane paths of seeing, meditation, and no-more-learning. Then, utilizing different skillful means and trainings, bodhisattvas and disciples attain nirvāṇa differentiated by their individual qualities.

This has briefly described the teachings of the lesser vehicle, which is like a staircase to ascend to the greater vehicle.

III

Although one may work thus for one's own benefit in this and future lives, due to a lack of great skillful means to benefit others, enlightenment is still quite far away.

One who makes efforts for the sake of others will achieve one's own purpose and also the purpose of others. How is it possible to gloriously fulfill one's own purpose if motivated only by the thought of one's own purpose, ignoring the purpose of others?

Is there any need to say more than this? Just look at the difference between a king who rules a kingdom well and one who cares only for gifts and riches.

Therefore in order to attain omniscience along with all sentient beings, take as noble refuges the following: the victorious one as a guide, he who has accomplished the two purposes, the sole teacher of all beings born out of an ocean of conduct and adorned with the purpose of others; the Dharma as the great vehicle by which buddhahood is accomplished, to be engaged in and stabilized; and the irreversible Saṅgha who are on the path to accomplish buddhahood. Take these as companions and to gather followers until one attains realization.

This becomes the foundation for practicing the jewel-like enlightenment thought that is the source of everything and outshines the excellence of saṃsāra and nirvāṇa.

A mind has no cause other than mind itself. Though momentary, it is not without cause. Mind itself is cause of mind. Therefore mind has absolutely no extreme of beginning. A sentient being, or "one with a mind," is so called because he possesses a mind.

As the sky has no limit, so is saṃsāra. Understand that even sentient beings living in saṃsāra are also limitless.

These sentient beings should be the objects of loving-kindness and compassion. Without choice they are suffused with severe suffering and wander endlessly in all the realms. The cycle of existence circles like a ring of fire. Thus it is called *cyclic existence.*

Although this is the case, beings' nature is the nature of the dharmakāya. Through skillful means they can become buddhas, but this will not come to pass with inferior familiarization and affinity, or inferior conducive factors and companions.

To abandon the purpose of others and not fully accomplish one's own purpose is mere liberation, which is called peace. The Buddha has said that this is a temporary result, like a city that emanates on the way to a monastery. Eventually all beings will become buddhas.

Loving-kindness is the wish that others may dwell constantly in the worldly and supramundane happiness of saṃsāra and nirvāṇa together with the stainless causes.

Compassion is the wish that others may be free from suffering and the cause of suffering, whether in saṃsāra, on the lesser vehicle, or in their resultant states.

Therefore always practice loving-kindness and compassion in this manner. If one has the thought of loving-kindness and compassion but hasn't engaged with skillful means, or if one has engaged but is not resolute, then these are still not for the purpose of others.

Thus the perfect Buddha is the fruition of perfect wisdom, compassion, and supreme power that eradicates all faults and has perfected all good qualities.

His attainment was also dependent on sentient beings, therefore aspire that you shall do likewise. This is wishing enlightenment mind.

With this thought, under the auspices of a spiritual master, take the vow in accordance with the formal ritual. This is wishing enlightenment mind.

Entering enlightenment mind is the intention to practice all the methods that accomplish buddhahood. Generating the resolution to do this is entering enlightenment mind.

As this is a method to generate that which is not generated and to increase that which has been generated, aspire to it with great joy and perfect entering enlightenment mind through practice.

A certain bodhisattva made the analogy that wishing enlightenment mind is like the wish to go, and entering enlightenment mind is like the actual act of going. Therefore reflect on methods of practicing the wishing and entering thoughts.

Only a handful can tell the various ways of differentiating between the mind and the enlightenment mind, and also between the wishing and the entering enlightenment mind, differentiated by practice. This is the relative enlightenment mind.

If examined, an entity is not unitary as it is interconnected. In the absence of the unitary, where is the multiplicity? What else could exist other than these two? Since there is no existence there is also no nonexistence. As these two contradict, neither is there both. As there is no basis of reason, neither is there not-both. Therefore under careful analysis, nothing can really exist. Even the mind also does not grasp at the sign. This is the cause that is similar to the ultimate enlightenment mind. This is also the view that is the supreme among all.

Familiarize yourself with this ultimate enlightenment mind after ascertaining it through analogies, through reasoning, and by remaining in meditative equipoise without any grasping.

Knowing the shortcomings of saṃsāra and nirvāṇa, do not aspire for them. Through recollecting the qualities of the Buddha, always aspire for them.

Feel joy in fulfilling the purpose of others through equalizing and exchanging oneself with others. This is the greatest skillful means to perfect the wishing enlightenment mind. Entering enlightenment mind is perfected through the accumulation of merit and wisdom. Practice it without discouragement or disappointment.

Perfect the Buddha's path by compassionately practicing all the six perfections without conceptualizing the three spheres and without procrastination or satiation. Fulfill completely all hopes of "those beings who are to be tamed by you" and place them on the stage of buddhahood. Endow all other sentient beings likewise.

The perfection of generosity has the intention of giving everything—material things, protection, Dharma, and loving-kindness.

The perfection of moral conduct has the intention to be free from any failing, to abandon faults, to accomplish merits, and to strive for the purpose of others.

The perfection of patience has the intention to be free from anger, to not cause trouble, and to ignore any harassment, and it is convinced that the Dharma is beneficial.

The perfection of effort has the joyful intention to gather merits through armoring, practicing, not being discouraged, and being unrelenting.

The perfection of concentration has the intention to not let the mind waver by turning the mind inward and away from all external objects and by placing the mind totally on mind itself.

The perfection of wisdom has the intention to know all by analyzing after comprehending the relative truth and by realizing that nature which is free of inherent existence.

Gradually all faults such as miserliness, immoral conduct, anger, laziness, distraction, and ignorance are destroyed, as the six perfections act as their antidotes.

Prosperity, birth in higher realms, pleasant physical features, fulfillment of aspirations, peace of mind, and being learned among all the wise are the temporary results.

The first five perfections continuously increase the accumulation of merit. The sixth fully completes the accumulation of wisdom.

In addition, the fifth is śamatha and the sixth is vipaśyanā. It is said that with an analytical mind that abides in calm, all remaining meanings can be grasped.

The former pacifies negative emotions and renders clear concentration and also clairvoyance. The latter eradicates all faults and completely perfects wisdom and primordial wisdom.

Moral conduct is the foundation of both calm abiding and wisdom. The remaining three are the conducive conditions for their accomplishment. If well analyzed, each perfection embodies the six perfections together with śamatha and vipaśyanā. Therefore realizing that each of them embodies the six and the two, constantly practice and familiarize. Buddhahood is then not far.

The four means of amassing disciples ripen sentient beings. Material gifts beckon all beings who are to be tamed and place them in temporary happiness. Pleasant speech correctly teaches the six perfections. Then guide them in right behavior, and cause them to be joyful because one's own actions are according to the meaning.

The first amasses disciples through material gifts and the remaining three through Dharma. The former benefits and the latter liberates. The purpose of others is completely included within these.

Gathering the two accumulations and putting effort into the two purposes should be carried out with the thought that everything is like an illusion. Familiarization in the practice without any conceptualization is the method of noble beings. Attempt to directly perceive enlightenment, which is like the nature of the sky, with a mind that is free of obscurations.

Merit and wisdom are the two wheels of a chariot. Skillful means is the wooden shaft, and vast vows are the supporting elements. The supreme horse endowed with the limbs of mindfulness, enthusiasm, and deep concentration gradually assembles one, two, three charioteers of aspiration and so forth, and enters into the path to liberation. This is called the path of accumulation.

Riding such a great chariot, you will gradually be endowed with the limbs of the five spiritual faculties and the limbs of the five powers. Fastening one and two elephants, enter into the well-differentiated path and reach the huge ocean of the wisdom of exalted beings. This is called the path of application.

Completely eradicate all thick faults on the path of seeing while traveling the stages and the paths. Like the radiance of the sky is reflected on the surface of the ocean, maintain the mind in the one taste of meditative equipoise and the dharmadhātu. The supreme shore of the ocean of primordial wisdom of the precious seven limbs of enlightenment is seen for the first time. Traveling toward it after seeing it is called the path of seeing.

The huge ship of nonconceptual wisdom adorned with the eight limbs of the banners of the noble path of enlightenment travels toward the shore of the peaceful dharmadhātu, blown by the constant and harmonious winds of the blessing of the Buddha. In the process, the ocean tides, which are like the faults to be abandoned through meditation, are all abandoned, and the bodhisattvas-in-training gain control over the precious Dharma of exalted beings. Familiarization through meditation with the meaning that was previously seen is the path of meditation.

In this way, crossing land and sea, just as you traversed the mundane and supramundane paths, enter the port of the island of the wish-fulfilling jewel. Now your voyage is complete; all unfavorable conditions are destroyed; all good qualities are perfected. Thus this path is called the path of perfection.

The supramundane path is also categorized in ten stages. Like ocean water is the same but appears differently depending upon the base, so the process of liberation is the same but categorized according to bases and qualities.

The stages are so called because each produces its qualities and acts as support for innumerable beings.

"Great Joy" is so called because it enters the stage nearing buddhahood and takes joy in generosity.

"Stainless" is so called because it is free from the stains of immoral conduct or broken moral conduct.

"Luminous" is so called because it is endowed with the light of the Dharma of scripture and the radiance of patience.

"Radiant" is so called because the fire that burns the faults of conceptual phenomena is ablaze with enthusiasm.

"Extremely Difficult to Conquer" is so called because it purifies those that are difficult to purify and guards the mind through concentration.

"Approaching" is so called because all the phenomena of saṃsāra and nirvāṇa are perceived directly through reliance on wisdom.

"Gone Far" is so called because it distances from the signs and excels through supreme skillful means.

"Immovable" is so called because it is not shaken by any conceptual thought and firmly abides in aspiration.

"Good Intelligence" is so called because it teaches the Dharma through four pure thoughts and great power.

The "Dharma Cloud" is so called as the cloud of concentration and mantras gathers in the sky of primordial wisdom.

Thereafter through vajra-like samādhi, the door to the precious treasure opens. Then this power transforms these four and buddhahood is attained, which is a treasure of immeasurable qualities and the only teacher or relative of all sentient beings.

Like clouds that disappear in the sky, the stains that are the obscurations disappear, and the dharmadhātu and primordial wisdom converge into one taste. This is called the natural body, the svābhāvikakāya.

Due to the power of immeasurable skillful means and compassion, great bliss and the five certainties of the pure realm, teacher, disciple, time, and Dharma are enjoyed. This is called the enjoyment body, the saṃbhogakāya.

The powers of knowing the right and wrong place, action, faculty, element, inclination, path of all goals, placing on liberation, recollection of places of past lives, recollection of birth and death, and eradication of defilements. These are the ten powers of the muni, the Lord Buddha, because like a vajra he removes all obscurations, the hordes of demons, and other opponents.

The Buddha has no qualms about teaching perfectly and accurately on relinquishment, primordial wisdom, the path of renunciation, and impediments. These are therefore the four fearlessnesses, because like a powerful lion he defeats opponents and prevails over disciples or beings who are to be tamed.

Free from erroneous speech and idle chatter; free from heedlessness and remaining in meditative equipoise; abandoning discriminating thoughts; having nonanalytical equanimity; without weakened aspiration, perseverance, mindfulness, or wisdom; and without weakened liberation and primordial wisdom, the physical, verbal, and mental actions are coupled with wisdom. Primordial wisdom knows the past, future, and present without obstruction. These are the eighteen distinguished qualities of the enlightened one, which are like the sky that pervades all yet is unstained by any. This is the quality of relinquishment. The good qualities are countless if categorized.

Understand that the ten faculties that are mentioned elsewhere are included within this.

The body is endowed with thirty-two marks of the ripened result for the purpose of others.

The feet are even and marked by wheels. Heels are broad and the toes are long. The toes are webbed with feet smooth and tender. The seven features of the body are prominent and the ankles are like those of an antelope. The private organ is concealed in a sheath and the upper part of the body is like that of a lion. Shoulders are broad, and the points of the shoulders are rounded. Hands are long and the supreme body is perfectly pure. The throat is stainless like a conch. Jaws are like that of a lion with forty teeth. The teeth are all the same size and evenly set, and the fangs are white. The tongue is long and endowed with excellent taste. The voice is like that of a kalaviṅka bird. The supreme eyes are deep blue in color with thick eyelashes. The precious hair is very white. The *uṣṇīṣa* is very high and cannot be seen even when peered at. The skin is thin and gold in color. The hairs grow to the right. The hair is the color of sapphire. The body has the proportion of a banyan tree. These are the thirty-two marks that excel those of powerful beings.

The eighty minor marks are elaborations of these. This is the glory of the rūpakāya.

Just as the full moon shines brightly among the stars on a very clear autumn night, the Buddha shines amid the tenth-bhūmi bodhisattvas.

And just like children become happy when seeing reflections of the full moon in the water, a buddha's appearance accomplishes the purposes, and merit is consistently accumulated. This is explained by following the instructions of the Mahāyāna sūtras.

Through the power of the saṃbhogakāya, in accordance with the merits of innumerable beings, the nirmāṇakāya appears in different forms and performs activities.

The svābhāvikakāya embodies the supreme primordial wisdom of the dharmadhātu. The saṃbhogakāya is none other than mirror-like wisdom.

The wisdom of equality and the wisdom of discrimination are its features. The wisdom of accomplishment embodies the nirmāṇakāya.

All these bodies and primordial wisdoms are consecutively the containers and contained. The purpose of oneself and the purpose of others, the subtle and gross, are laid down similarly.

The Buddha is also ever unceasing: being the same flavor as the dharmadhātu, born out of an inexhaustible cause, destroying all unfavorable factors, fulfilling all aspirations, gaining power to overcome all, and because the objective of his activities is without end.

His teachings will also continuously remain in this mundane world. There is no appearance and nonappearance, rising and settling, increasing and diminishing. It is taught that what is seen arises because of conceptual thought and the power of karma, and not because of the condition of the locality.

Likewise the sky and the sun are both seen to appear and to disappear, but in reality it is not actually so. Similarly, the Buddha continuously blesses pure yogis. Wonderful they are indeed, engaged always in the festival of the nectar of Dharma.

This is a brief oral teaching of the Mahāyāna tradition. For more, learn from others for the sake of the unsurpassable great purpose. This ends the third part, which explains the Mahāyāna tradition.

Conclusion

If the Dharmic path for worldly beings is followed, then the god realms are not far. Further, if you climb the staircase of gods and humans, then liberation is very near.

It is said that all the results that are gained through the three yānas are the result of the one yāna. So I have explained here in accordance with the sequence of meaning.

In fact, the noble assembly, which has realized emptiness, and also the very learned have illuminated the teaching again and again in many different ways. Here I have explained briefly and concisely, as advice for you to consider and also for the benefit of others.

May the wise forgive me for any mistakes in this text as my mind is like a child's. I haven't studied all knowledge extensively, and I have taught incoherently. By this merit, may all beings lead a proper worldly life and become buddhas by entering the door of Dharma.

A Garland of Jewels, a collection of advice to Prince Gibek Timur, was composed by Chögyal Phagpa at the great Sakya Monastery on the eighth day of the *guwu* month in the Male Fire Tiger Year. It contains 204 stanzas.

NO POSTAGE
NECESSARY
IF MAILED
IN THE
UNITED STATES

BUSINESS REPLY MAIL

FIRST-CLASS MAIL PERMIT NO. 1100 SOMERVILLE, MA

POSTAGE WILL BE PAID BY ADDRESSEE

WISDOM PUBLICATIONS
199 ELM ST
SOMERVILLE MA 02144-9908

5. Teaching on *A Garland of Jewels*

His Holiness Kyabgon Gongma Sakya Trichen Rinpoche

Whenever you receive teachings, the first thing to do is always to create the right motivation. Think that for the sake of all sentient beings, who are as numerous as space is vast, one must attain full enlightenment. Think that it is for the sake of attaining enlightenment that one is receiving this profound teaching, and think that after receiving it one will diligently follow the path. It is important to receive teachings with the right conduct. This means the body should be respectfully seated, the voice silent, and the mind concentrated on each and every word of the teaching.

The actual title of this teaching is *Advice Given by Drogön Chögyal Phagpa*. Drogön Chögyal Phagpa and his uncle, Sakya Paṇḍita, were among the first Tibetan masters to travel to China. They turned the wheel of the Vajrayāna teachings there for the first time, to the benefit of an immense number of beings. During this period, Chögyal Phagpa bestowed many profound empowerments and teachings upon the emperor's family. He also wrote teachings addressed individually to the princes and to other members of the royal family. Although there is no clear record, I believe that these teachings were given as parting gifts just before he returned from China to Tibet.

During that period, the great dynasty of the Mongols, which was known as the Yuan dynasty, ruled a vast empire that included many parts of Asia and extended as far as Europe. Among the royal family was a crown prince named Gibek Timur, and it was for him that Drogön Chögyal Phagpa composed this book of advice, which is informally known as *A Garland of Jewels*.

Homage Verses: Preparation and Praise

> **Prostrations to all buddhas and bodhisattvas.**

Every teaching begins with paying homage by performing prostrations to the excellent ones, so that the author will be able to compose the text without any obstacles and so that those who are studying the text in the future will likewise be able to overcome obstacles. Paying homage to all the buddhas also demonstrates that the author is a holy practitioner, so that his followers and those who will study the text in the future will similarly follow virtuous ways. For these reasons, all texts begin by paying homage with prostrations to the buddhas and bodhisattvas. In Tibetan, the word for homage is literally *prostrations.*

In the next verse, the author pays homage specifically to the Buddha:

> **Prostrations to the Buddha, who is like Mount Sumeru and whose magnificent body is born from an ocean of merit and wisdom, adorned with unfathomable qualities.**

This verse develops the simile of Mount Sumeru, which is said to arise out of the ocean. Mount Sumeru is vast, and it contains the essence of all the elements. It possesses great good qualities like jewels and so on. As Sumeru is born out of the vast ocean, so a buddha is born out of a great accumulation of merit and wisdom. According to the Pāramitāyāna, the Buddha attained enlightenment because he accumulated an enormous amount of merit over the duration of three countless eons. He also accumulated an enormous amount of wisdom. He studied, contemplated, meditated, and finally achieved complete realization of the ultimate truth. Upon attaining enlightenment, he parted from every type of obscuration and gained an enormous number of good qualities. Therefore the author pays homage to the Buddha and performs prostrations so that through the Buddha's blessings he will be able to compose this book of advice without any obstacles.

Born in the land of oceans of merit; splendid in race, wealth, and physical appearance; competently ruling country and subjects: may you have victory, glorious jewel-like prince.

He praises the prince, comparing him to a jewel. Again, jewels come from the ocean; jewels are splendorous and fulfill one's wishes. Like a jewel, the prince was born from an ocean of virtuous deeds. He accumulated vast amounts of merit in previous lives due to which he has been now born as a human being. Furthermore, he has been born as a prince in a lineage of powerful emperors. He possesses the splendor of wealth, power, and glory. He fulfills the wishes of his subjects and looks after the welfare of the country. When he says, "May you have victory, glorious jewel-like prince," he is praising the prince and also making aspirations for him.

I, Phagpa, possess a base of pure moral conduct and uphold great teachings like an ocean abounds with precious jewels. From my ocean-mind the words of this teaching arise like a garland of jewels illuminating every direction with its radiance, an ornament beautifying both self and others. This is offered with a virtuous mind.

Drogön Chögyal Phagpa is himself a fully ordained monk and a bodhisattva. He keeps the Mantrayāna vows and maintains very pure moral conduct. This is one of the good qualities needed to compose texts. He has also heard and studied many great teachings—so many that his mind is like an ocean abounding in jewels. He has gained great qualities through his pure conduct and through study, contemplation, and meditation, acquiring great inner understanding like a wealth of jewels. Out of this ocean of his mind, the words of the text are said to arise like a garland of jewels. This garland's radiance illuminates in all directions; it is a very precious teaching.

The teachings are said to be virtuous in the beginning, virtuous in the middle, and virtuous in the end. Their virtue in the beginning is that when you hear the teachings, you learn what are the right things to do. We learn that it is wrong to indulge in nonvirtuous deeds that arise from negative minds, because the negative emotions are the source of our suffering. We do not know this without study. Although nobody wants suffering, at the same time we do not know where our suffering comes from. But by studying the teachings, we learn how suffering arises. It arises from our own negative emotions and not from anything external.

After learning this, you should contemplate, study, and analyze the teachings. In this way, you deepen your knowledge of the sources of suffering and the thought that you don't want to experience suffering. It isn't a matter of merely praying, "May I be able to overcome suffering." We must act. We have to suppress the negative emotions so that they do not become active. This is how the teachings are virtuous in the middle.

Finally, after you have studied and contemplated, you should meditate. Only through meditation will you be able to dig out the roots of negative thoughts so that they will be totally eliminated. Thus the teachings are virtuous in the end. The teachings are radiant, and they illuminate in all directions. Chögyal Phagpa offers this to the prince with a good aspiration, a good motivation, and a virtuous mind.

The next part explains the purpose of giving this advice.

> **What is the point of making material gifts to one with such immense wealth? Instead, I offer this gift of Dharma to illuminate, like moonlight at midnight opens the kunda flower.**

There is no point in making a material gift to a crown prince who is extremely wealthy and powerful. Instead, Chögyal Phagpa offers this gift of Dharma. The prince is already very knowledgeable; actually, he already knows the Dharma. Nevertheless, it is worthwhile to teach it to him again in order to enhance and improve his knowledge.

Part I: Worldly Advice

> **Possessing a wealth of worldly riches but lacking the riches of Dharma is like enjoying delicious food that is mixed with poison and only begets suffering.**

Spiritual practice is very important. One may have great wealth and power, and the glory that comes with wealth and power, but if one lacks the Dharma then no matter how prosperous or powerful, and no matter how grand or glorious one may be, eventually these things will cause suffering. No matter how high you are, no matter how powerful you are, no matter how strong you are, it is all going to end one day. These glories are like eating delicious food mixed with poison. You enjoy the delicious flavor, but it will create great pain and suffering in the future. It is very important to combine worldly prosperity with Dharma prosperity. With both together, you will be able to fulfill your purpose in both this life and in future lives. Practicing the Dharma also not only benefits you, but it benefits others as well. You will fulfill your own purpose and the purpose of others.

Conversely, possessing the riches of Dharma but lacking worldly wealth is like an encrusted gem that cannot serve the purpose of others.

True practitioners who lack worldly power or worldly prosperity cannot really do great things to serve the purpose of others. One may be a very good practitioner, but this alone will not benefit very many people because one cannot reach or affect many people. A prince, however, has the well-being of thousands of people in his hands, and by using his worldly power he can lead them according to the Dharma. He can be a person with spiritual as well as political authority. In order to benefit the greatest number of beings in this lifetime, worldly prosperity is a great help.

However, by possessing both types of wealth, the purposes of both self and others can be accomplished, like a well-cut jewel that beautifies both self and others.

If you have both worldly power and Dharma qualities, you can serve the purpose of yourself and accomplish your own benefit because you know and practice the Dharma and lead a virtuous life. You will also be able to reach many other people, just as a powerful prince can affect the lives of many thousands of people. In this way, the purposes of both oneself and others are served. This is likened to a jewel that has been well cut so it becomes very precious and is appreciated by everyone. To have both worldly and spiritual good qualities is as beautiful as a well-cut jewel.

> **Therefore, in order to render fruitful the two glories with which you are endowed, I have carefully considered these words.**

Having thought in this way about the benefits of possessing both kinds of wealth, and having considered what would be of great advantage to the prince and others, Chögyal Phagpa has given this advice. He requests the prince to listen to this teaching very carefully, to the words as well as their meaning.

Next, the actual advice begins:

> **If even the brilliance of the sun, the depth of the ocean, and the loftiness of Mount Sumeru will disappear at the end of time, what need to mention the wealth of sentient beings?**

These things—the sun, the ocean, and Mount Sumeru—appear to be very stable, vast, and permanent. These are symbols of everything apparently strong and everlasting. We never think that the sun will fall from the sky, that the oceans will dry up, or that Mount Sumeru will disappear. But everything is in fact impermanent. The Buddha said that all compounded things are impermanent, which means that anything that depends upon cause and conditions for its existence is impermanent. One day even the sun will disappear, and all will become dark. The oceans, although very vast and deep, will disappear. And Mount Sumeru, although very large and very stable, will also disappear.

It is said that Mount Sumeru is the essence of all the elements. Bardo spirits, who have no physical bodies, can travel through the world very quickly and without hindrance, just as our minds can go to a place merely by thinking of it. At the moment, right here, for example, my mind could be in India or in China. Similarly, bardo beings can travel extremely quickly to very distant places. But bardo beings cannot go through very holy places like Bodh Gaya, and they cannot go through the wombs of mothers unless they have the necessary karmic link. Bardo beings likewise cannot pass through Mount Sumeru because it is the combined essence of all the elements. It is very powerful and very stable.

All of these things will disappear one day. Everything is impermanent. What then to say about our worldly riches? No matter how much wealth we have, no matter how much power we have, no matter how many relatives we have, no matter how clever we are—all of this will be of no use in the end. When we leave this world, all of this is gone. Sentient beings are like bubbles floating on the surface of water, bubbles that can burst at any time.

> **Realizing this, do not be arrogant because of your immense wealth. Always rely on mindfulness in order to increase the gloriousness of your glory.**

Realize that all compounded things are impermanent and that worldly prosperity is impermanent and has no essence. Never be arrogant. Emperors are very powerful and thus have the potential to become very arrogant. Especially in ancient times, they could do whatever they liked. They could play with the lives of people. Chögyal Phagpa is advising this future emperor not to be arrogant because none of this—none of the glories or the power—is permanent.

Even the bright sun that illuminates the world, the deep oceans, and Mount Sumeru will disappear. What of your life, your glory, and the prosperity that you possess? Do not be arrogant, and in order to increase the gloriousness of your glories, be very mindful, knowing that everything is impermanent, that all compounded things are impermanent, that all contaminated things are suffering. It is said that people must have something to fear. Without fears, one will do whatever they like, and this is not good. Therefore be careful and be mindful of the right and wrong ways to act.

> **Having tasted suffering, develop renunciation. Even happiness is subject to change. Everything conditioned arises out of a cause. Perceiving that this cause is the cause of suffering, do**

not let your mind be defiled. Bend your mind to become the condition for the accumulation of merit through experiencing the afflictions of oneself and others.

Realize that all of saṃsāra is suffering. Remember that suffering is of three kinds: the suffering of suffering, the suffering of change, and the suffering of the conditioned nature of all phenomena. The suffering of suffering is what we normally think of as suffering, things like physical pain and mental anxiety. In our human realm, no one is free from the sufferings of birth, old age, sickness, and death. There are many other sufferings, as well. Even those who have wealth experience mental suffering, and of course those who do not have wealth experience physical sufferings such as the lack of food, clothing, and so on. We experience sufferings such as legal problems, family problems, relationship problems—so many different kinds of suffering, and there is no end to it. This is the suffering of suffering.

The suffering of change results from the happiness that we normally consider to be joy. When you compare joys with sufferings, they appear to be happy, but they are also another form of suffering. For example, a person who is living in a poor condition—in a very poor house that lacks heating and cooling, that lacks water and is smelly and filthy—if moved to a house with all the modern facilities will feel very happy. But this happiness is only because he was previously living in a very poor condition. If these facilities were the real source of happiness, then it would be the case that the longer he stayed there, the happier this person would become. However, if he stayed in that room with those facilities for an extremely long period of time, he would again feel unhappy. He would want to go somewhere else, do something else, and experience something new. He would not want to stay in that house forever and ever, even with all the modern facilities. A prison cell with all the amenities is still a prison cell. Any happiness is subject to change.

Everything is conditioned. The conditioned nature of all things guarantees that our very existence in saṃsāra is the third type of suffering. No matter where we go or what we do, there is no real satisfaction. Countries that are poor have a lot of problems. Things malfunction, and you cannot just do what you like. Everything takes a long time and is very slow. Everything is very complicated, and so one suffers and complains. Then, when you go to a country that has new facilities and is very modern and efficient, you also suffer. The pace is too fast, there is no peace. There is no satisfaction. That is the suffering of the conditioned nature of all phenomena.

Knowing these three sufferings—the suffering of suffering, the suffering of change, and the suffering of the conditioned nature of all things—Gibek Timur should resolve not to allow his mind to be defiled. He must act to control his defilements. A defiled mind creates nonvirtuous deeds and these deeds create all types of suffering. He should therefore try to accumulate merit, and not by himself alone, or for himself alone. Because he is a leader of many people, they will follow whatever he does, and he should lead them in the practice of virtue.

> **It is through the confluence of merit and prayer that your body, directly and indirectly, came into being from your father's and mother's lineage. Therefore reflect on their kindness. By cultivating a virtuous way of life, your hereditary lineage will flow like a river, and, having concern for your subjects, your wishes will be fulfilled.**

Gibek Timur's position, his high birth, even his body, are not things that just happened accidentally. They happened because of causes and conditions. Through meritorious deeds, he created good karma, prayed, and made noble aspirations. He has been born into the emperor's family with no cause other than his own virtuous deeds, prayers, and merits.

Chögyal Phagpa also reminds him that his own father and mother were very kind, especially his mother who gave him his life and his body. A baby cannot survive without a mother, as it can neither eat nor talk nor survive by itself. But he was taken care of by his parents and by other relatives, too, and he should remember this. He must remember the kindnesses that they showed him, and think of how to pay back their kindness and the benefit that he received.

By doing such virtuous deeds, his hereditary lineage will continue and be stable, like a river continues to flow. People will respect and admire him. He should proceed in a virtuous way and lead the people in virtuous ways, so that his own lineage of emperors will continue and he will win the hearts of millions of people and fulfill his own and their wishes. The state will be very stable and powerful, and the people will be happy. In this way his own glory will be accomplished.

Having depended totally on the Buddha's glory, make known his kindness, venerating him always like a jewel on your crown. Just as he, like a jewel, bestows upon you fulfillment of each and every need, similarly you will also be worthy of others' veneration.

The prince's happiness, joy, and glory are all due to the blessings of the Buddha who taught the Dharma. Remembering this, he must venerate, respect, and be devoted to the Buddha, who is like the jewel on top of a crown resting atop a king's head. The Buddha is the source of all glory, prosperity, and happiness because the Buddha taught the Dharma, and following the Dharma brings the benefits of joy, prosperity, and glory.

By following the Dharma, one's aspirations will be realized as if one had in one's possession what is called a wish-fulfilling jewel. It is said that there is a jewel that if you clean it and place it atop a banner, and then make prostrations and offerings to it, all one's wishes will be fulfilled. Such a jewel can bestow food, clothing, shelter, medicine, and any type of material need. By following this righteous and virtuous way of life, and by leading other people in virtue, the result will be that the prince will receive the benefits of respect and veneration.

Among the various types of people, be considerate of, respect, and care for the elderly among your subjects, the truthful among speakers, the authentic tradition among traditions, the altruistic among ascetics, the wealth of wisdom among the various types of wealth, the wise among the respected, the destitute among the inferior, the sick among the destitute, the one who follows you among your spouses, the one who will carry on your lineage among sons, the one who never deceives you among

relatives, the one who benefits you among friends, the one who obeys your orders among attendants, the one who repays your kindness among those whom you have benefited, the one able to remain patient among those whom you may have harmed, the one who suddenly appears among all. Through this, others will be inspired and also engage in moral conduct.

The "elderly among your subjects" means that among the old, the young, the middle-aged, poor, rich, and so on, one should respect the elders because they not only have more years, but they also typically have more wisdom because as the years go by, they acquired more understanding.

"Truthful among speakers" means to respect those who speak the truth, and the "authentic traditions among traditions" refers to the Dharma. When we choose a material purchase, we usually give it some thought and we ask others for their advice before we make a decision. Well, the Dharma is something that is not only for a little while, not only for this lifetime, but for many lifetimes. If we choose wrongly, it will be wrong for many lifetimes, and it will be a very great mistake. We must choose carefully the authentic Dharma.

Sakya Paṇḍita explained the five qualities of authentic Dharma: first, that the teachings were given by the Buddha. Second, that they were collected by the Buddha's disciples. Remember that in the Buddha's time there was no writing, let alone recording devices like tape and video. The Buddha's disciples were very wise, and when the Buddha gave teachings they observed very carefully and many teachings were learned by heart. After the Buddha entered mahāparinirvāṇa, the disciples held three gatherings to remember and collect his teachings. Whatever teachings that were remembered, each one of them was recited, first one and then another and another. This was the first gathering, and it wasn't until after the third gathering that the Buddha's teachings were written down. This is why the second quality of the authentic Dharma is said to be "gathered by the gathering." The third quality is that the teachings were explained by the paṇḍitas, very learned persons; their equivalent in modern times is persons with doctoral degrees. The fourth quality is that the teachings were meditated on by the mahāsiddhas. Finally, because the teachings came from India to Tibet and they had to be translated, the fifth quality is that the teachings were translated by genuine translators.

Teachings that have all five of these qualities, according to Sakya Paṇḍita, are genuine Dharma. Such teachings should be heard and studied, contemplated, and practiced. There are many different kinds of teachings that claim to be the highest, to be very profound, and so on. But just saying the word *highest* or *profound* doesn't prove anything.

"The altruistic among ascetics." There are many different kinds of practices, behaviors, and conduct. Those who are altruistic—meaning genuine in helping others—should be respected.

"The wealth of wisdom among the various types of wealth." Material wealth is not reliable. It can be snatched from you by people who are more powerful; it can be stolen by thieves; it can be wrongly used; it can be wasted. If, for example, parents leave material wealth for their children, there is no certainty that this wealth will benefit them. It may be wasted or used in the wrong way. It may become a source of fighting or misery, and so on. But the wisdom that parents teach their children cannot be taken from them and cannot be stolen by thieves. It will remain in their minds, not only in this life but also in the next, and it will continue to benefit them. Therefore among all types of wealth, the wealth of wisdom is the best.

"The wise among the respected." There are many different objects worthy of respect due to their title, power, helpfulness, or whatever. Among them, the most respect should be accorded to those who are wise. Wisdom is like the light that dispels the darkness of ignorance. Wisdom gives real strength and pride.

"The destitute among the inferior." There are many different kinds of people classified as inferior, but among them, those who are destitute need to be protected and should not be neglected.

"The sick among the destitute." There are likewise many different kinds of destitute people. Some are materially poor, some lack wisdom, and so on. Among the destitute, those who are physically ill should be the object of the greatest compassion and should be cared for.

"The one who follows you among your spouses." Among one's spouses or potential spouses, one who follows you in your ideas, who is like-minded and sees things in the same way, creates a situation that is harmonious.

Spouses who have different ideas and different tastes will find it much more difficult to be in harmony.

"The one who will succeed your lineage among sons." Traditionally, sons carry the family lineage and the family name. Among sons, remember first the ones who carry the hereditary line and the family name. In Tibetan, *bu* is the general term for sons; it can also refer to children, both sons and daughters. Any child who will carry the family lineage, the family tradition, the family line, should be given more care.

"The one who never deceives you among relatives." One can have many different kinds of relatives. There are those who are far or near, helpful or not so helpful, and so on. Above all, show consideration and respect to those who are not deceptive and whom you can trust.

"The one who benefits you among friends." Friends can be classified into those who are helpful or not; those who help you when you are in need, and those who do not. When you are successful, you will find many people want to be your friend. Friends and relatives will come to you, but when you are not successful they will all go away. These are not the right kind of friends. Real friends are those who do not deceive you and who will help you when you are in need and have problems.

"The one who obeys your orders among attendants." One can have many different kinds of attendants. Some do not follow what you say and have their own ideas. They want to do things their own way, but a good attendant follows what you say and what you order, wanting to do things just as you say.

"The one who repays your kindness among those whom you have benefited." Often, when you help people, instead of paying you back or reciprocating, they do the opposite and hurt you. Among those whom you have helped, look for the ones who return your favors and who reciprocate when you benefit them.

Up to this point, this has been advice for the worldly level. The prince will become emperor one day and will have to look after the kingdom and many subjects. Therefore he will need this wordly advice.

"The one able to remain patient among those whom you may have harmed." Sometimes people get hurt even when you don't have the intention of hurting anyone. For example, a certain action or word may cause a misunderstanding causing people to feel hurt. Those who fight you back immediately are not good. Those who are able to bear the feeling of being hurt and yet remain patient are the people to be cared for.

"The one who suddenly appears among all." This is also one of the samaya of the kriyā tantra. In olden times, travel was very difficult. For example, you had to carry all of your food, and it was very difficult to find a place to stay, and so on. Especially those on long journeys encountered many difficulties. Travelers who appear suddenly are the ones who are most in need. To care for them by giving them shelter, clothing, food, drink, or whatever they need is among the kriyā tantra samaya.

"Through this, others will be inspired and also engage in moral conduct." If the prince does the right thing, then his subjects will follow his example and also lead virtuous lives. If he does wrong things, then his subjects will do likewise, and there will be turmoil.

Fishermen, butchers, and the like who harm others will never accomplish their own purpose. What need to mention their accomplishing the purpose of others?

Here, Chögyal Phagpa is talking about those whose livelihood involves performing nonvirtuous deeds, for example, by constantly slaughtering or torturing animals or humans, and so on. Everyone longs for happiness, and they do such work for the sake of their own happiness. And yet these people will not in fact fulfill their own purpose; they will not find happiness through a career of performing nonvirtuous deeds. If they cannot accomplish their own goal of happiness for themselves, how can they accomplish happiness for others?

The inferior, middling, and superior levels of the disciples, bodhisattvas, and victors are determined by the extent of their benefit to others. Although this is not obvious, you can identify a small, medium, or great lord because he will be benefiting others in a small, medium, or great way.

The disciples are the śrāvakas and pratyekabuddhas. Next are the bodhisattvas, and "victors" refers to buddhas. The buddhas are at the highest level, the bodhisattvas are middling, and the disciples, or śrāvakas and pratyekabuddhas, are at the inferior level. The Buddha benefits all, and therefore he is the greatest. Bodhisattvas benefit many beings, and so they are medium. The śrāvakas' aim is to obtain the peace of nirvāṇa, and for this reason they are inferior. The reason that the Buddha is excellent, that the bodhisattvas are medium, and the śrāvakas and pratyekabuddhas, or disciples, are inferior is entirely based on the extent of their activities to benefit others.

This is not something immediately known to us. We learn it through the texts rather than by seeing it. However, even in our own worldly experience we can see that among leaders, those who benefit others the most are the greatest.

Therefore if you have loving-kindness toward all sentient beings, what need to mention the obligation to have loving-kindness toward those who depend upon you?

In the bodhisattva's way of life, you are supposed to benefit all sentient beings because you realize that all sentient beings are your own mother and that they have benefited you very much. It is very important to generate loving-kindness in this way toward all sentient beings, including your own most hated enemies. When you think this way toward all beings, obviously, you also need to benefit your own subjects and those who depend upon you for their well-being. It is very important to generate loving-kindness toward all sentient beings.

Know that all the lives that depend upon you are equal. It is not the way of the Dharma to satisfy a few people by killing others.

To each person, their own life is very precious, and this is true for everybody. Just as my life is precious to me, so it is for every sentient being. Ending one's life means losing everything that you have in this life. I have been told that in ancient times in China, if the emperor did not like you, he could give an order to kill not only you but also all your relatives for nine generations, or something similar. This was done due to the fear of someone taking revenge. Innocent relatives were killed just to prevent acts of revenge.

> **Sensually delightful activities, free of defilements, gratify many. Though you may indulge at appropriate times to be rid of boredom, under careful reflection, know that it creates a cause of suffering to indulge unwisely in temporary pleasures by harming others. Realizing this, abandon such actions.**

A ruler of a country charged with looking after the state's welfare sometimes becomes very tired and bored. Therefore Chögyal Phagpa says that it is permissible for him to enjoy himself as on a holiday. Sometimes ordinary people go for a holiday and do things such as hunting or fishing. If one goes only to track animals without harming them, this is allowed in order to overcome boredom at the appropriate time.

However, it is harmful to be a habitual enjoyer, or someone who hunts just for the enjoyment of harming other living beings. This creates one's own suffering. Everyone longs for their own happiness, but due to ignorance we create further causes of our suffering. Knowing this, Chögyal Phagpa instructs the prince not to do such things now that he understands this.

> **One constantly makes mistakes oneself yet does not tolerate the faults of others. There is no contradiction greater than to kill the innocent for this.**

Drogön Chögyal Phagpa was against capital punishment. Here he says that no one is perfect; no one has only good qualities. Also, people who are full of faults also have some good qualities; they are not 100-percent faulty. No matter who you are, you may make mistakes. If you are unable to bear other's mistakes—if, let us say, you are a very powerful emperor and you kill someone because they do something that displeases you—there is no greater contradiction than this and it is totally wrong.

> **One will become an inspiration by showing compassion, be worshiped by caring for others, and be praised by speaking pleasantly. Such is the reality of phenomena.**

The meaning of this verse is obvious. Virtuous deeds are the real cause of your happiness and joy, and the accomplishment of all your wishes. When you practice compassion for beings—for example, when you love even an animal, such as your dog, the animal will be very happy, want to be with you, try to help you, and show that he or she likes you. If you are kind to people and show them compassion, then you will win their respect. If you care for them when they have problems or when they are in need, giving them food, clothing, medicine, comfort, encouragement, and consolation, then in turn they will respect you and worship you. If you speak pleasant words, you will likewise be praised.

This is obvious, and we can see throughout history that leaders who are very selfish, violent, and cruel will be hated and despised even after their death, but leaders who are caring and compassionate are respected after their death. In recent history, we see this in a person like Mahatma Gandhi. From the outside he looked quite poor. He was very thin and he wore very poor clothing, very simple cloth, and he went barefoot or wore simple wooden sandals. But he was very compassionate, cared for people, and earned their respect. I have heard that even many very powerful British generals respected him very highly and saw in him something very different and extraordinary.

> **Shouldn't the practices of loving-kindness and accomplishing others' benefit also be engaged by those striving only for this worldly life, no need to mention for the sake of enlightenment?**

In order to attain enlightenment you need to generate compassion and benefit others. Of course, it's clear that without compassion you cannot gain virtuous qualities because compassion is the life force of all virtuous qualities. In order to attain enlightenment you need to generate great compassion and loving-kindness toward all sentient beings. Otherwise, bodhicitta, or enlightenment mind, has not arisen. Bodhicitta arises through compassion and loving-kindness. In order to attain enlightenment, these practices are absolutely essential. However, even at the worldly level, the more you show compassion and the more you benefit others, the more you will be respected.

> **Realizing this, practice loving-kindness and the benefit of others. This will accomplish one's own and others' purpose in this and the next life.**

For the purposes of this life, for example, to rule a country well, it is very important to generate loving-kindness and compassion and to benefit beings. Knowing this, always be compassionate and help others. This will also accomplish benefit for your subsequent lifetimes because the practice of virtue will continue to benefit you throughout future lives.

> **Hardship is necessary to increase one's lifespan, wealth, and Dharma practice. If any of these are not going well, overcome the difficulty through persistence.**

To increase your life, your wealth, and your Dharma practice, you must bear difficulties. Kings and rulers in the past lived very luxurious lives, and it was difficult for them to do lengthy practice. Even today, rich people are quite used to a luxurious lifestyle, and it is difficult for them to recite prayers and meditate for a long time. However, by going through these hardships, you will gain great benefit, and by seeing the benefit you will become able to bear it.

For example, when a business man sees that a great profit can be obtained, he will proceed no matter how difficult or complicated the task. It is difficult to keep moral conduct, study, contemplation, meditation, and so on. However, by doing these things you will bring the benefits of a long life, wealth, and, of course, the Dharma. You will prosper in this life and experience benefits in the next life, too.

> **Understand what scholars have said: wealth protects the retinue, the retinue protects the body, the body protects life, and all of them protect the Dharma.**

The retinue means, I think, the people around one: attendants and associates. By giving them various benefits, they are protected. They in turn protect one's body and one's life. All of them together protect the Dharma, which is the most important thing. Wealth and so on can protect material things and the body, but the Dharma is very important because it protects the mind.

> **Even though at times, certain religious or worldly pursuits may be unsuccessful, do not be discouraged. Look at the actions of businessmen and farmers.**

Emperors have many affairs and there are many things to be done, both worldly and Dharmic activities. It might not be possible to accomplish everything, but in order to accomplish some things, one must not become discouraged. No one can accomplish everything, and sometimes we are successful and sometimes we fail.

Do not be discouraged when you fail, thinking, "Now I can't do anything." You must simply do it again. The examples are a businessman and a farmer. If a businessman fails at one business, he does not stop; he tries to start another one and become more profitable. Similarly, a farmer does not stop if this year's crops fail. He simply tries again next year. Likewise, you must do the same.

> **It is extremely difficult to accomplish an important task all at once, but even the hardest can be accomplished by undertaking it gradually, like the case of an ant and its nest.**

Difficult tasks and big projects are hard to accomplish all at once. Proceed gradually and with determination, even though you may encounter many problems, challenges, and difficulties, and even if you sometimes become discouraged. Try not to be discouraged, and keep working gradually and continuously. If you do things very vigorously and you fail, and then you stop trying due to the failure, then, of course, you will never achieve success. No matter how many difficulties or problems you face, you must go on, proceeding continuously. No matter how difficult the project is, if you do it continuously, you will be able to accomplish it. The ant is a very small animal, but it can create a huge anthill.

> **Many opposing factors arise when undertaking a substantial task, and even a single arrow alone is enough to kill.**

When undertaking a very large, important, and beneficial project, even a single opposing factor that is harmful to the project is a thing too many. Even one obstacle or hindrance is too much and can cause great harm. The example is that even one poison arrow can kill you. One problem can damage the whole project

> **Beneficial actions, like the atoms of an ocean, are never too plentiful; wouldn't the king of a larger kingdom be correspondingly greater?**

Things that are beneficial are never too many, even if they are as numerous as the atoms in the ocean. It cannot be said that there are too many good things.

> **Possessing skillful means, even harmful beings can be won over, like a hook that tames a wild elephant and renders it serviceable to the world.**

When running the affairs of state, skillful means are necessary. If you have skillful means, even those who wish harm to you can be brought over to your side. Harmful beings can be won over; enemies can become friends. Those who oppose you can become your helpers if you have the skillful means to do it. The example is a single hook that can tame wild elephants, making them serviceable for riding and other things.

> **Though worldly beings say enemies should be pacified through violent means, peaceful means can pacify—it's just like fire to fire and water to water.**

In the worldly way of thinking, when someone harms you, you take revenge. If someone declares war on you, you declare war on them, and destroy your enemies by violent methods. Chögyal Phagpa here explains that violent methods do not work, but peaceful methods do. Peace can make peace, but violence cannot produce peace. His Holiness the Dalai Lama actually gave this advice to George W. Bush! When he met him, he said that you cannot really pacify your enemies through violent means, but you can through peaceful means. The example Chögyal Phagpa gives is that if you are burned by fire, applying fire to the burn is one of the traditional treatments. Or if water enters your ear, you can pour more water into it and thus draw it out. Likewise, to make peace you have to be peaceful; you cannot make peace through violence.

> **Although a single harmful being may be subdued by violent means, *one* will only increase to many. This is similar to what happens to the pebbles of the riverbank when some are removed.**

You can destroy an enemy with violence, but things will not stop there. We earlier talked about the Chinese emperors who understood that if you kill a person, you must be concerned about his family, associates, and others who will want revenge, so your enemies will multiply. This verse says that by destroying one enemy through violence, you will create more enemies. The example is the pebbles in a riverbank of a river: when you scoop them away, immediately more pebbles come.

If through skillful means you can multiply those in your favor, you will become more stable, just as a house built upon a solid mountain is more stable.

If you pursue peaceful methods with your enemies, making friends of them instead of using violence, then not only your enemies but your enemies' relatives, friends, and associates will also become your friends. The more friends you create, the more stable your authority will become. The example is a house built upon rock. I think this is a very good piece of advice.

Overcoming opposition in this manner, rule those under your power religiously because Dharma brings happiness to the world.

Through violence you cannot destroy your opposition or enemies, but through skillful means you can conquer people and countries. Those who are conquered should be ruled according to the Dharma so that everyone will be happy in this life, and so that in their future lives they will continue to experience happiness. The manner in which to rule is further addressed in the next verse:

Rule the country and subjects kind-heartedly, speak pleasantly, confer titles accordingly, and fulfill material needs generously.

To rule a country and to rule your subjects according to the Dharma, remember that everyone wants happiness. You must love them in the same way that every mother loves her child and wishes her child to be physically healthy and mentally happy. A mother also wishes her child to be continuously happy, which is to say that she wishes her child to have the causes of happiness. You must give this same love.

Also, you must speak pleasantly. We say in Tibetan that although speech has no sharp edges, it can cut people's hearts. You may have a kind heart, but if you say harsh things, people will become upset.

You should also give your subjects titles, gifts, and awards according to the work they have done and meet their material needs. Then people will be happy, and because they are happy, as loyal citizens they will follow you and your commands.

> **By ruling in this way, your wealth will increase like rain that falls upon all the guests gathered at a party. Does not the farmer reap what he has sown in his field?**

If you rule in the way described, virtuously pursuing peace, increasing the country's wealth, and working for peoples' benefit, then their increase will in turn increase your own wealth, and their benefit will become your own benefit. Everything will come back to you; all the benefits that you have given will also fall upon you. The example is a farmer who reaps what he has sown in his fields.

> **Although all the subjects are equal, you should punish those who are not lawful and reward those who are. This is like an illness and the strength of the body.**

You must treat all your subjects equally. In modern political systems, everyone is considered to be equal under the rule of law, whether you are a president or a beggar. But in the past, things were different. The king was more or less the highest authority and he made the law. Chögyal Phagpa tells the prince that he should rule all his subjects equally. At the same time, those who break the law and do the wrong things should be punished. Otherwise there will be even more lawbreakers, until the country is ruined. Also, those who follow the rules and are loyal should be rewarded.

The example he gives is illness. If you have an illness, it must be treated or the disease will harm you. Punishing those who are breaking the law is like treating an illness. Those who are doing good things should be rewarded; they are like the strength of the body that should be maintained.

> **Punishments should be given only in order to rehabilitate: scolding, beating, confiscating, and condemning. The death sentence should never be handed down. The wise wash dirty**

clothes and wear them again. Who would think it wise to dispose of them by burning?

Chögyal Phagpa is very much against capital punishment. Here he uses clothes as an example. Those who do wrong things are like dirty clothes. When dirty clothes are washed they readily become good, clean clothes. But if one burns them because they are dirty, they can never be worn again and are gone forever. Likewise, the death sentence may eliminate the lawbreakers, but at the same time those subjects will be gone forever. This is not wise. If you treat them well, lawbreakers can become good people.

Give recognition according to actions, and take it away if it is not appropriate. Reflect on the different ways of presenting food to babies, children, and adults.

Those who work hard and accomplish a lot should be rewarded with awards and titles. Those who do mediocre work should be given mediocre rewards, and it is not right to give big rewards to those who do only a little work. Chögyal Phagpa gives the example of different kinds of food given to different kinds of people. If you give adult food to a baby, the baby cannot digest it. If a baby's food is given to an adult, he will not be filled.

A person without any good qualities and a person without any faults do not exist in this world. Examining what is frequent and what is infrequent, accept a fire torch even though it is smoky, abandon poison even though it is tasty, and use a horse cart while on the ground and a boat while in the water.

Among ordinary people, there is no one who has only good qualities and is without any faults. Only the Buddha is perfect. An ordinary person, no matter how good, still has some faults. Also, no matter how bad a person is, they will still have good qualities. After carefully examining them, accept the person who has more good qualities and fewer faults. The example is a torch. When a torch burns, it produces smoke. But it also gives light and is useful, so we accept the smoke. People who have more faults and fewer good qualities should not be accepted. The example is like delicious poison. It is very harmful even though it is tasty. One should also judge persons according to the occasion. When you are traveling over land you need a horse, and when traveling by water you need a boat.

> **Understand that there are four kinds of wealth: wealth that is like an enemy, wealth that is like one's relative, purposeless wealth, and actual wealth.**

He says that there are four kinds of economics. Sometimes wealth is like your enemy because it gives great trouble and causes problems.

> **First acquired and accumulated, then increased and protected, finally becoming harmful through quarreling and infighting— this is wealth that is like an enemy.**

What is wealth that is like an enemy? In the beginning, when you are acquiring it, you experience great difficulties, and you go through a lot of pain and anxiety. In the meantime, when you are increasing it and protecting it, you are worried all the time. You worry that someone will snatch your wealth from you, steal it from you, or take it away from you. And all this time the wealth does not give you joy or happiness, only pain. In the end, it becomes a source of fighting. People—even relatives, even brothers and sisters—often fight over property and money. They quarrel and may even kill each other. I myself have seen this. That kind of wealth is just like an enemy. It has no benefit.

> **Wealth that is honestly obtained, effortlessly accumulated, and given with a virtuous mind: such wealth that creates benefit is wealth that is like one's relatives.**

Relatives are always helpful; family will help you. Some wealth is like this. In the beginning, when you acquire this wealth, you do not experience great pain. Sometimes people acquire wealth quite easily because of their previous karma. They do not need to go through much pain, worry, and anxiety. Some wealth is obtained through nonvirtuous deeds, which is not good. This wealth, however, is acquired effortlessly and through virtuous means. Then, after obtaining it, because of your virtuous mind and good aspirations, you make offerings to the Buddha, Dharma, and Saṅgha, and you give to the poor and the needy, the destitute, the sick, and so on. It gives benefit to many people continuously, and it also increases. This kind of wealth is like a relative.

One of our lamas once told me that in the beginning he was quite poor and he tried to accumulate wealth. He had been quite stingy, and he tried to collect every bit of money that he could, but he was never able to accumulate much money. Later, he tried to give money, spend money, make offerings, and give to people in need. It was then, he said, that he accumulated some money. Being stingy, you do not accumulate money, but being generous you can.

> **Wealth obtained through means that are neither good nor devious, wealth that is neither given nor used, but is only hoarded all the time and then dissipated, such wealth is wealth without any purpose.**

Some wealth is gained without much difficulty and not gained through nonvirtuous activities, but then once you have it you are very stingy. You do not give it away, and you do not use it for yourself either. Instead, you only collect and collect and collect, trying all the time to save money.

There was a news story in India. A bank clerk worked for many years. He was a very, very stingy man—so much so that he wouldn't even spend money to buy his own food. Instead, he would go to places where he could receive free medical treatment, free food, and so on. He spent all his life this way, saving everything and never spending money, until, of course, the day came that he died. The man had no relatives or family members, and no plans to benefit any cause, and so the government took the money, and that was that.

Obtained at the beginning either with little or much difficulty, the wealth that is utilized by oneself and for others for temporary comfort, such is the actual wealth.

This is what we might call ordinary wealth. It might be acquired in a virtuous way or in a nonvirtuous way, with much difficulty or not, and it may be used for your own comfort or spent on relatives, friends, and so on—not necessarily for offerings. This is "actual" or general wealth.

Among these, always abandon the first and the third. Always use the second, and use the fourth as wished.

The first—wealth that is like an enemy—should be avoided. The second—wealth that is like a relative—should be increased and pursued. The third wealth is wasted and purposeless wealth. Again, one should avoid it. The fourth wealth one may pursue as wished or as is appropriate. In this way, Chögyal Phagpa gives very good advice in financial matters.

Indulging without any contentment begets suffering. Understand how decline of strength and indigestion arise.

It is not good to practice overindulgence, to spend a lot of money, to be extravagant, or to show off your riches by wearing expensive clothes or using expensive things. It causes suffering. If you eat extravagantly, by eating too much or by eating foods that are too rich, you will experience indigestion. By overspending and overindulging you will likewise create suffering. You should avoid this. Instead, follow a middle way. This is the Buddhist philosophy. To be very ascetic is wrong because it will hurt your physical body, but to be very extravagant is also wrong.

Alcohol causes one to be despised by others, ruins one's body, weakens one's intelligence, ruins purpose, and separates one from the spiritual path. Therefore always look upon alcohol as a poison.

This is very good advice. In Tibetan, the word translated as "alcohol" is *chang*, the name of a beer made from barley, but it applies to any kind of alcoholic drink.

He names all the faults of alcohol. First, one will be despised by others. We used to have a doctor in the Rajpur area, a very good doctor. His diagnoses were very good, and he had a lot of experience, but he drank a lot. He drank so much that people would recommend that you go to see him early in the day, before lunch, because after lunch he wouldn't be able to make good diagnoses. In Tibet we used to have carpenters and tailors who did very good work, but when they were drinking they did everything wrong, making wrong cuts and so forth. If you drink like this, you will be criticized by others, even despised. Second, alcohol ruins one's body. It causes many diseases, like cirrhosis of the liver. Third, alcohol weakens one's intelligence. When you are drunk, you become like a mad person, not knowing the right way from the wrong way. People who are ordinarily good people, who can talk and think clearly, will not be able to talk or think clearly. Fourth, alcohol ruins one's purpose. When you cannot talk or think, how can you do your purpose? Fifth, it separates one from the spiritual path. Obviously, if you cannot even do worldly activities properly, how can you follow the Dharma path?

Any kind of alcohol, any kind of intoxicant, should be avoided, and you should look upon them as poisons. I think that today this means any kind of drug that can ruin your body or your mind. It is especially good advice for young people. It is very wise—very good—to say no to drugs.

> **Moreover, attachment to sensual objects depletes the merits accumulated and always undermines one's capacity. Therefore always rely on contentment.**

Attachment to the sensual will decrease your merits. It is always better to have contentment, and one must be very careful not have strong attachment.

> **Even when conducting an activity, it is wise to carry out only after examination, and foolish to examine after performed.**

This is found in the scriptures of the noble beings. Carry out every action only after examination and discussion, and you will fulfill all your goals. Even if it turns out otherwise, there will be no regrets.

Whatever you undertake to do, before you begin the project or the work you must examine it to discover what is the nature of the activity, what are the goals or the desired outcomes, and so on. After careful examination and discussion, then you can proceed. That is the wise way to carry anything out. The foolish way is to do it and discuss it later. Whatever you do, it must be examined and discussed before undertaking it. And once begun, you must carry on until the end. You must discuss it with friends and especially with wise people. If you proceed this way, then even if the work is not ultimately accomplished, you will not have any regrets.

In short, be neither arrogant when wealthy nor downcast when impoverished. Repay kindnesses to those who serve you well. Venerate those worthy of veneration, and protect the weak. Exercise control over other territories and rule your own lands and subjects according to the Dharma. Utilize wealth with alertness and accomplish activities in a noble way.

When you are wealthy or successful, you should not be arrogant; when you are not successful and when you are downcast, you should not be discouraged or timid. Those who have served you and those who have done good things should be recognized for their kindness. Your parents, teachers, elders, and the wise should be venerated, and the weak, poor, destitute, and sick should be protected. Exercise control, and rule your land and your subjects according to the Dharma.

In Buddhist teachings, there is the law of karma. I think that all of the major religions including Christianity describe in some way a law of cause and effect. I know that Hindus emphasize it very much. The Buddha, who possessed omniscient wisdom and knew each and every cause and effect, explained it in great detail. In Buddhism it is said that the whole universe, the whole of saṃsāra, is caused by karma.

There is virtuous and nonvirtuous karma. Those who are born in the lower realms got there from nonvirtuous karma. Whatever karma you have committed, you will have to take the result. You cannot avoid it. Even though your actions may have been done for somebody else, that person will not gather the result. Only the one who committed the karma will get the result, and the karma will never disappear; even after eons, it will remain. It will chase you wherever you go, and the reward or punishment will only go to the person who committed it.

Another classification of karma is into three kinds: strong, weak, and very weak. Strong karma, either good or bad, will ripen in this very lifetime. Weaker karma ripens in the next life, and very weak karma ripens after several lifetimes.

Karma is very subtle.

There are what are called "throwing" karmas. If I throw something here in this room, it will land perhaps outside the window or in a corner of the room. Likewise, the karma that is the cause of our being born here is "throwing" karma. It is the karma from a previous life that landed us here in this human life. We may have been in a hell realm or in a deva realm, and the good karma that threw us here into the human realm and in America was the throwing karma.

Then there is "completing" karma. After being born here in the human realm, some people have a very good life, a long life with prosperity and success, and so on. That is called good "completing" karma—the throwing karma was very good, and also the completing karma was very good. Some people, even though they are born into a higher realm like the human one, face many miseries there. They may have a short life and suffer from sickness, poverty, the lack of success, and all kinds of miseries. In this case, although the throwing karma was positive, the completing karma was negative, and therefore they experience the miseries.

Similarly, for beings in the lower realms, their throwing karma is negative such that they have been born into a lower realm; however, sometimes even in the lower realms one's completing karma is quite good. This is especially so with animals such as pets—especially pets in America, where some animals enjoy better lives than some human beings living in developing countries. Their completing karma is good karma such that they enjoy a luxurious existence even though they are in a lower realm.

To rule the country according to the Dharma means to rule according to the law of karma. Understand that negative deeds, either by the king or by the citizens, will cause suffering, while virtuous deeds will bring benefit.

"Utilize wealth with alertness and accomplish activities in a noble way." If you use your wealth primarily for enjoyment and for your own purpose in an extravagant way, this is not right. Not using your wealth at all, hoarding it, is also not right. You should follow a middle way. This is the wise way and the noble way, through which you will be glorious and prosperous. When a king rules in a Dharma way, the country will be prosperous, and everyone will be happy.

Part II: Beyond-Worldly Advice Concerning the Lesser Vehicle

By doing like this, one will be glorious and prosperous in this world. Through this, tread the path of Dharma in order to gain the happiness of worldly life.

While we are in this world, and when we are happy and prosperous, we should think toward the beyond-worldly level and how we can find happiness there. The way to do this is to enter the path of Dharma. If you are unhappy here, if you are not successful, and if you have a lot of pains and a lot of anxieties, then you cannot begin the Dharma path in the right way, just as a person who is sick cannot do much for himself. The first thing is to have a good and healthy body and a healthy mind, to have peace and calm. On the basis of this, one will be able to turn to the beyond-worldly level, meaning beyond this life. In order to find happiness that continues in this life and beyond this life, one should follow the Dharma path.

Although the text does not mark it, this is where the second section begins. Up to this point, he has given advice on how to lead a worldly life and how to rule a country according to virtuous ways and the Dharma. Next, he teaches the actual Dharma.

There are many teachers, and each one guides along a different path. Even though there is only one teacher who has eliminated all faults and the causes of those faults and who has perfected all good qualities and is supreme, no one would say, "I have little knowledge" or "I am full of faults." Discern each teacher's qualities from his character and teaching.

The Tibetan word translated here as "teacher" is *tönpa*, which means "guide." This word is used to refer to the founders of various religions. There are many guides or founders who lead their followers along different paths and in different schools. The highest founding master and the surest guide is one who has eliminated all faults including the causes of those faults and who has perfected all good qualities. Such a teacher is supreme.

Of course, every founding master claims that they are the greatest. Chögyal Phagpa explains that one must use one's own intuition and intelligence to find out which founding master is the greatest. By studying his conduct, character, and teaching one can discern whether or not a teacher has eliminated all faults and perfected all good qualities.

A teaching that is free from any stains of spoken or written mistake, that is completely substantiated by the two valid cognitions, that completely abandons contradictions and inconsistencies, and that brings certain benefit and happiness belongs to a noble tradition. A master who discovers on his own such a noble tradition is supreme among masters, and those who follow his teaching also become noble.

Just saying that the Buddha is great does not establish that this is true. The Buddha is great because of his teachings, which are free from the stains of spoken or written mistake.

We can also substantiate them through the two kinds of valid cognition, the two valid means of knowing. One means of valid cognition is cognition based on reasoning or proofs. For example, we can validly know that there is a fire on a mountain if we see smoke; the smoke proves that there is fire. The other is direct perception; cognition through personal experience.

Those who follow the Buddha and his teachings are called the Saṅgha. They, too, must be noble and great, because of the greatness of the teachings. And if the teachings of the Buddha are understood to be great, then the Buddha will be established as an authentic founding master, one who has eliminated all faults and gained all good qualities. In this way we establish the authenticity and nobility of the Three Jewels.

> **Followers who practice with pure faith in the Buddha, the bodhisattvas, the Dharma, and disciples are noble. Therefore you, too, realizing the good qualities of the Buddha, the Dharma, and the Saṅgha, in order to be rescued from fear, should faithfully take the teacher, the path, and the companions as the ultimate refuge as long as you live.**

As I have said, the primary thing is the Dharma. Because the Dharma is pure, and because we can establish its validity with valid cognition, and because it has no contradictions, we can experience real confidence or belief in the Dharma. We can establish a real feeling of faith or trust—not blind faith, but faith based upon good reasons. Our thinking should not be, "I am Buddhist, and therefore I have faith in the Buddha." Instead you must come to understand that because one can receive great benefits from the Dharma, because the Dharma can eliminate all of our faults and develop the great qualities of buddhahood, it is virtuous in the beginning, middle, and end.

In your own experience, the Dharma can give so much comfort and so much benefit. It is because of this that it is possible to have faith in the Buddha. Such wonderful and profound teachings can only come from a great teacher. Because of our faith in the Dharma, we have faith in the Buddha and in his heirs, the bodhisattvas. Bodhisattvas are called heirs or sons of the Buddha because they hold his lineage and because eventually they become buddhas, just as your own children who hold your hereditary lineage and will one day hold your place. The disciples are the śrāvakas and the pratyekabuddhas. These will not become buddhas; they follow the Buddha's teaching, but instead they become arhats.

The Buddha, his sons, and the disciples are all great. When one knows the great qualities of the Buddha, the Dharma, and the Saṅgha, then with faith in them and fear of continuing to suffer in saṃsāra one takes refuge in the Buddha as one's guide, in the Dharma as one's path, and in the Saṅgha as one's companions on the path. There are three kinds of faith: clear faith, believing faith, and desiring faith, and the motivation described here is mostly believing faith.

If, for example, you want to go to a place that is unknown to you, the first thing you need is someone to show you the correct way, someone with knowledge and in whom you trust. This is how you should take refuge in the Buddha, as a guide to show you the path to liberation. Next, in order to reach your destination, you must travel yourself and undertake the journey; the guide cannot just place you there in your destination. You must practice the Dharma, which means taking refuge in the Dharma as the path. Finally, you also take refuge in the Saṅgha. When you undertake a long and difficult journey, if instead of traveling alone you go with trusted companions, then it is a great help. You take refuge in the Saṅgha as your companions. The duration of taking refuge in the Buddha, Dharma, and Saṅgha, according to the Śrāvakayāna tradition, is for as long as you live.

> **This is the great foundation of all good qualities capable of clearing away all faults. Thus entering the door of Dharma dependent upon the supreme refuge, always act according to the Dharma, whose foundation is moral conduct.**

Taking refuge is the first step by which one enters the Dharma path. It is the root of all the Dharma. It is the preliminary practice of the entire path, and it is also the foundation of all the vows. Refuge is what differentiates Buddhists and non-Buddhists. Being born into a Buddhist family does not make one a Buddhist. Anyone—regardless of their family—who takes refuge in the Buddha, Dharma, and Saṅgha for the purpose of obtaining liberation becomes a Buddhist. Taking refuge is the great foundation of all good qualities and clears away all faults. After taking refuge and entering the door of Dharma, one should always act according to the Dharma.

Refuge is also known as a primary ground. Just as the earth is a foundation for all things animate and inanimate, pure moral conduct is the foundation of the arising of all good qualities.

> **Be wholesome by keeping the eight-limbed vows of a lay practitioner for a day and night. The Buddha has said that one will be born as a heavenly being of the desire realm by practicing ethical discipline.**

Moral conduct has many different levels. Here the focus is on eight-limbed vows for lay practitioners. The eight limbs comprise three branches. The first branch is called the branch of moral conduct. It includes, first, abstaining from killing any living being, from the tiniest insect on up; second, abstaining from stealing, from insignificant things up to very precious things; third, abstaining from lying; and, fourth, abstaining from sexual activity. These are the four limbs of moral conduct of the first branch. Next is the branch of attentiveness. This consists of abstaining from intoxication, meaning alcohol or any other kind of drug. The third branch is the branch of ascetic practices, which includes avoiding sitting on a high seat, abstaining from eating after midday, and abstaining from singing, dancing, and wearing jewels or cosmetics. These are the eight precepts.

A "day and night" means one twenty-four-hour period. If you keep the vows every day, you are known as a pure upāsaka. If, as this verse describes, you do not keep them every day but only on special occasions such as the full moon day and the new moon day, you will become accustomed to moral conduct, and in the next life you will be able to be reborn in the heavenly realms and in the realm of desire.

> **Abide by the precepts of individual liberation in order to abandon attachment, which causes future rebirth, to abandon objects of distraction, and to maintain pure moral conduct.**

The main causes of birth in the cycle of existence are attachment and karma; in other words, desire and deeds. These are the causes of being born again and again in saṃsāra. When you see that all saṃsāra, whether one is born in a lower realm or in a higher realm, is entirely suffering, and you earnestly wish not to be born again, the first step is to abandon the cause of rebirth, which is attachment.

You must also abandon objects of distraction. When this life is finished, attachment, deeds, and distraction will cause us to be born into our next life. In order to leave this cycle, you must abandon the cause of the cycle. The first step is to abide by the precepts, the individual liberation vows, or prātimokṣa, which are rituals according to the Śrāvakayāna and Pratyekabuddhayāna. Good moral conduct is very important, and of course there are many different levels of it.

> **If you are not able to uphold all the precepts, hold any according to your ability. Upholding even a single precept enhances your practice of moral conduct. When it becomes familiar, virtue will naturally increase without difficulty.**

Ordinary people very accustomed to a worldly way of life may not be able to keep all the precepts. Therefore the Buddha, who was very skillful in his teaching, provided many different levels of vows. For example, if you cannot keep all the precepts, you can become what is called a "one-precept holder," for example, by taking the first precept to abstain from killing. One who keeps two, abstaining from both killing and stealing, is known as a "some-precept holder." One who keeps three—say, by abstaining from killing, stealing, and lying—is called a "most-precept holder." One who keeps all five precepts—abstaining from killing, stealing, lying, sexual misconduct, and intoxication—is known as a full upāsaka.

Although full upāsakas must abstain from sexual misconduct, when keeping the eight precepts for a single day, one abstains from any kind of sexual conduct or activity at all.

Keeping even just one precept brings great benefit, and slowly you become able to keep more and more. In the beginning, virtuous conduct may be difficult, but as you become accustomed to it, it will become easier and virtue will increase.

> **To become learned in all knowledge and to become liberated, incline your mind to listen; extensively study and discuss various types of logical reasoning and traditions. Those who are learned in all fields of knowledge, particularly possessing the ability to discriminate well, never make the mistakes of accepting what is wrong and rejecting what is right.**

After establishing oneself in good discipline, which is the foundation of all good qualities, the next step is to study. You should study, listen, and discuss the teachings extensively. You must use your own intuition and intelligence to find out whether the Buddha's teachings are genuine according to your own life experience. Only then, and not because of mere blind faith, should you take the teachings as your path. To do that, use your own intelligence and wisdom. You need to study and acquire knowledge. You need to listen, study, discuss, analyze, and examine. After you have gained wisdom, then you can decide what should be rejected and what should be accepted.

> **Particularly listen to teachings without becoming satiated by extensive Dharma. Dharma is the essence of knowledge and the means to greater wisdom and merit. With a doubting mind it is difficult to fulfill one's own purpose. Similarly, if you listen but don't understand the meaning, it is difficult to fulfill one's aim. Therefore analyze what you learn with valid reasoning and you will be able to ascertain the meaning clearly, as your eyes can see objects clearly.**

You must study all the sciences—all the different kinds of knowledge—but especially the holy Dharma. The word *dharma* in Sanskrit has many meanings depending upon the context. Here it refers to the holy path that leads to liberation and enlightenment. For the Dharma, you must study very carefully without ever deciding that you have studied enough. Even though you may have already heard a teaching, you should always listen tirelessly, because the holy Dharma is the essence of all knowledge. This will increase your wisdom and merit.

It is very important to think, analyze, and clear away doubts. When your mind is filled with doubt, you cannot accomplish anything. In the Buddhist tradition, it is important to analyze what you are taught and to utilize your own reason, intuition, and wisdom, and to do this repeatedly. There are two different kinds of disciples. Inferior disciples follow the path because of faith, but superior disciples follow based on their own reasoning. Eventually, through analyzing the teachings, you will be able to ascertain their meanings clearly, just like seeing objects clearly.

> **Thus through dedication in listening to teachings and analyzing them, little by little your wisdom will increase, like a honeycomb is built by honeybees.**

There are many things to study, but you should not become discouraged. Continue to study again and again. Even if your efforts are small, your knowledge will increase, just like tiny water droplets can accumulate into oceans. Likewise, the bee is a very tiny creature, but it can build a huge honeycomb.

> **These are the skillful means for mastering the teachings. Just as grain is harvested through effort, so realization is attained through study.**

The holy Dharma has two aspects: teaching and realization. Studying, listening, and analyzing the meaning of the teachings is the skillful means by which one attains mastery of the teaching aspect. On this basis, the realization aspect is attained. The teachings are the cause of realization.

> **By ascertaining the suffering of saṃsāra and its causes, which are karma and negative emotions, one increases virtuous actions.**

Through study, you can ascertain the suffering of saṃsāra. The cause of suffering is twofold: the defilements, or negative emotions, and deeds, or karma. When you know this, you will increase your virtuous actions, and do other practices.

> **By remaining in meditation analyzing the repulsiveness of the body, loving-kindness, interdependent origination, categories of elements, mindfulness of inhalation and exhalation of breath, and objective and subjective phenomena, one will attain the happiness of the higher realms.**

Different practices address different types of defilements. For example, as an antidote to attachment to and desire for one's own and others' bodies, one can practice meditation upon the repulsiveness and ugliness of the body and its dirty aspects. Thinking that it is made of very dirty things—such as meat, bone, blood, and so on—can lessen one's desire or attachment.

Then as an antidote to anger, meditate upon loving-kindness. This is done by thinking that all sentient beings, just like oneself, wish to be happy. All sentient beings have the same feelings. Next, as an antidote to ignorance, meditate upon interdependent origination, or causes and their effects. Next, because our minds have so many thoughts and we cannot control them, meditate on concentration upon the breath and then also on objective and subjective phenomena. By doing these different practices for the different defilements, one will become able to control the mind and attain the happiness of the higher realms.

> **Then traverse the worldly paths of accumulation and application, and the supramundane paths of seeing, meditation, and no-more-learning. Then, utilizing different skillful means and trainings, bodhisattvas and disciples attain nirvāṇa differentiated by their individual qualities.**

These are the five paths we've explained before, which lead us to the Buddha's level. Whether one becomes a buddha or an arhat depends upon the methods used, and bodhisattvas and disciples are differentiated by their qualities.

> **This has briefly described the teachings of the lesser vehicle, which is like a staircase to ascend to the greater vehicle.**

After the section of worldly advice, Chögyal Phagpa gave the section of beyond-worldly advice, which began with a description of the Śrāvakayāna path, then continues to the Mahāyāna path. One begins at the worldly level, then proceeds to the Śrāvakayāna, and then to the Mahāyāna.

Part III: Beyond-Worldly Advice Concerning the Greater Vehicle

> **Although one may work thus for one's own benefit in this and future lives, due to a lack of great skillful means to benefit others, enlightenment is still quite far away.**

The first section of the text was about this life and how to be a good human being and lead a virtuous life. The second section was about the Śrāvakayāna path and how to attain nirvāṇa. Thus it did not talk very much about other beings. However, even if you try your best to achieve liberation and be free from the suffering of saṃsāra, without the skillful means to help other beings, ultimate enlightenment will still be very far away. The sole purpose of attaining enlightenment is to benefit others. If you lack this enlightenment mind, then you cannot achieve enlightenment.

> **One who makes efforts for the sake of others will achieve one's own purpose and also the purpose of others. How is it possible to gloriously fulfill one's own purpose if motivated only by the thought of one's own purpose, ignoring the purpose of others?**

In worldly existence, from beginningless time until now, we have thought only of ourselves and our own benefit. In this life, day and night, we make efforts for our own sake and yet have never succeeded in fulfilling our own purpose. The buddhas, who totally devoted themselves to the benefit of others, accomplished both purposes—the benefit of themselves and the benefit of others. Although nirvāṇa is a great thing when compared to saṃsāra, which is full of suffering, nirvāṇa is a place or a state in which good qualities are not fully developed. In order to fulfill one's own purpose and fully develop one's own good qualities, one must think of the purpose of others. This is the Mahāyāna path. If you lack the means to help others, you will not be able to fulfill your own purpose. It is very important to devote your energy, time, and effort for the benefit of others.

> **Is there any need to say more than this? Just look at the difference between a king who rules a kingdom well and one who cares only for gifts and riches.**

A king who rules the whole country and who benefits the entire country and all of his subjects is a glorious and great king. He is not at all like one who cares only about his own riches and about money for his own personal use.

> **Therefore in order to attain omniscience along with all sentient beings, take as noble refuges the following: the victorious one as a guide, he who has accomplished the two purposes, the sole teacher of all beings born out of an ocean of conduct and adorned with the purpose of others; the Dharma as the great vehicle by which buddhahood is accomplished, to be engaged in and stabilized; the irreversible Saṅgha who are on the path to accomplish buddhahood. Take these as companions and to gather followers until one attains realization.**

One enters the Mahāyāna path for the sake of completely fulfilling one's own purpose or benefit. In order to achieve your own purpose, you need to devote yourself to the purpose of others. You need to enter the Mahāyāna path because mere nirvāṇa is not worthy of attachment. The teachings tell us that all sentient beings are our mother, our father, and our relatives, and that to abandon them and ignore them, seeking liberation for oneself alone, is not right. Therefore it is very important to enter the Mahāyāna path.

The Buddha is born out of the bodhisattva's way of life. To be a bodhisattva means to ignore one's own purpose and to devote one's full energy, effort, and time to the purpose of others. When you do this, you will obtain the highest result, and in order to do it, the very first thing—the root of all the Dharma, the preliminary practice for the entire path, and the foundation of all the vows—is to take refuge.

Every school of Buddhism practices refuge, but the Mahāyāna refuge has four special characteristics. First, the cause: generally, the cause of taking refuge is threefold: fear, faith, and compassion. Although all three causes are part of the Mahāyāna refuge, the main cause is compassion. When you enter the Mahāyāna path, the sole purpose is to save all sentient beings from the suffering of saṃsāra and to lead them to the path of happiness. Without compassion you will not be able to do this.

Second, the objects of refuge—the Buddha, Dharma, and Saṅgha—are the same in all schools of Buddhism, but the Mahāyāna refuge teachings explain them differently. In the Mahāyāna, the Buddha is described as possessing three kāyas: the dharmakāya, the saṃbhogakāya, and the nirmāṇakāya. We take refuge in the Buddha, as the guide who shows us the path. The Buddha eliminated all forms of obscurations and gained every possible realization, and is therefore victorious from every point of view. We take refuge in the Dharma as the path. The Dharma is what saves us, because although the guide is important, only a guide is not enough. The guide can show you the path but you must travel it yourself. This is why the Buddha said, "You yourself are your own savior. Nobody else can save you." This is why Chögyal Phagpa said the Dharma is "to be engaged in and stabilized." And when you engage in the Dharma path, you need trusted companions for your journey. Thus we take refuge in the irreversible bodhisattvas. So the Mahāyāna refuge objects are understood this way: we take refuge in the Buddhas who possess the three kāyas, in the Dharma that is both the Mahāyāna teachings and the realization obtained by the buddhas and bodhisattvas, and in the Saṅgha composed of the irreversible bodhisattvas.

The first distinguishing characteristic of Mahāyāna refuge is the cause, which is primarily compassion. The second is the object, explained above. The third characteristic is the duration, which is until enlightenment is won. And the fourth characteristic is the purpose, namely, for the sake of all sentient beings. In the Mahāyāna, the aim is to attain full enlightenment for the sake of all sentient beings.

> **This becomes the foundation for practicing the jewel-like enlightenment thought that is the source of everything and outshines the excellence of saṃsāra and nirvāṇa.**

Taking refuge is the foundation of all the vows. After taking refuge, one should establish bodhicitta, or enlightenment mind, as one's motivation. Enlightenment mind is like a precious jewel that is the source of all happiness and benefit. There is no other virtuous deed higher than creating enlightenment mind. It is the real jewel of the mind. Producing this thought just once is like the fire at the end of an eon; it can burn away all negative deeds. Enlightenment mind is also like a brave hero because when you are traveling on a very dangerous path, there is no need to have any fear when you are accompanied by a strong and heroic companion. Enlightenment mind is like a wish-fulfilling tree that grows inexhaustible fruit because no matter how much you pick, more fruit is always growing. Enlightenment mind is the only way to overcome all suffering. There is nothing greater than it.

> **A mind has no cause other than mind itself. Though momentary, it is not without cause. Mind itself is cause of mind. Therefore mind has absolutely no extreme of beginning. A sentient being, or "one with a mind," is so called because he possesses a mind.**

Mind is very different from other kinds of entities. Other entities are visible to the eye, they can be touched, and so forth. They are made up of the elements, and they can be described in terms of their color, shape, and so forth. However, the mind cannot be seen. It cannot be touched.

Its color, shape, or size cannot be described. It cannot be located or said to be here or there. The mind, therefore, cannot arise from the elements or from visible things. Mind only arises as the continuity of mind itself; from the mind comes mind.

Furthermore this mind is forever momentarily changing. The mind is not a unitary entity; it is always different. What we thought yesterday and what we think today are not the same. We often refer to beginningless time, meaning that the mind has no beginning. Surely this is one of the great wonders, that this continuity of mind has no beginning.

> **As the sky has no limit, so is saṃsāra. Understand that even sentient beings living in saṃsāra are also limitless.**

Space, or the universe, has no limit, and saṃsāra likewise has no end. No matter how many sentient beings one rescues, no matter how many sentient beings attain liberation or enlightenment, the number of sentient beings never decreases. If space had limits and you took seven steps to the east, then of course you would be seven steps closer to the east and seven steps farther from the west. But because space is infinite, there is nothing in regard to which you become nearer and nothing in regard to which you become farther. Similarly, although countless beings are rescued or attain enlightenment, the number of sentient beings does not decrease. And as long as there are sentient beings, the Buddha's activities will continue. A buddha's activities never cease. As long as saṃsāra remains, the Buddha's activities also remain.

> **These sentient beings should be the objects of loving-kindness and compassion. Without choice they are suffused with severe suffering and wander endlessly in all the realms. The cycle of existence circles like a ring of fire. Thus it is called *cyclic existence.***

All sentient beings in saṃsāra are objects of our loving-kindness and compassion. All beings long for happiness. Whether you are a believer or nonbeliever, whatever views you hold, it is certain that nobody wants suffering and every being longs for happiness. However, each one, because of his or her individual karma, his or her own actions, experiences great suffering. This is called the wheel of life. The wheel turns one rotation and then another begins, and it keeps going forever. Saṃsāra goes on and on, and it never ends. An individual, or an individual mind, has an end, but saṃsāra does not. As an example, think of a seed. The seed grows and produces another seed, and this goes on and on. Although we cannot point to a beginning for this process, we know that if we burn the seed, there will be a definite end.

> **Although this is the case, beings' nature is the nature of the dharmakāya. Through skillful means they can become buddhas, but this will not come to pass with inferior familiarization and affinity, or inferior conducive factors and companions.**

There is a vast difference between ordinary sentient beings and fully enlightened beings. Sentient beings are beings who are helpless, who lack knowledge and wisdom, and who through their ignorance create karma and the causes of suffering, even though their aim is to be free from suffering. This experience, this process, goes on and on. Buddhas are beings who are fully awakened, who have fully eliminated all forms of obscurations, and who will never acquire them again. The difference between ordinary beings and buddhas is like the difference between the sun and darkness.

However, the mind, in its basic nature, is not different from the dharmakāya of buddhahood. The nature of sentient beings' minds and the nature of the Buddha's transcendental wisdom is the same. The dharmakāya is not something gained from outside oneself. The dharmakāya is something already within our own minds. It is something we already have that is not yet known to us or seen by us because it is covered with obscurations. Because the true nature of the mind of all sentient beings is pure, every sentient being has the potential to become a buddha, just like every seed has the potential to grow into a crop if it meets with the right conditions.

> **To abandon the purpose of others and not fully accomplish one's own purpose is mere liberation, which is called peace.**

The Buddha has said that this is a temporary result, like a city that emanates on the way to a monastery. Eventually all beings will become buddhas.

Every sentient being can become a buddha if he or she meets with the right methods. However, because of differing propensities, the presence of superior or inferior conducive factors, and different companions, all beings cannot be led to buddhahood straight away. Thus the Buddha has given different teachings that suit different kinds of sentient beings. He has established three different vehicles, or yānas: the śrāvakas, the pratyekabuddhas, and the bodhisattvas. The first two, the Śrāvakayāna and the Pratyekabuddhayāna, are not vehicles to the ultimate goal of buddhahood. They are like way stations or places that one encounters on a long journey where one can rest. Eventually, of course, everyone will become a buddha.

Loving-kindness is the wish that others may dwell constantly in the worldly and supramundane happiness of saṃsāra and nirvāṇa together with the stainless causes.

Bodhicitta, or enlightenment mind, is the source of all benefits and all fruits or results. Enlightenment mind arises from loving-kindness and compassion. Loving-kindness is the wish that all sentient beings be happy and have the cause of happiness. Loving-kindness is demonstrated in the way that every mother loves her child and wants her child to be physically healthy, mentally happy, and to have continual happiness. All of us have a natural tendency toward loving-kindness. This is true whether we have heard the teachings or not. We want people to be happy and to possess the cause of happiness.

Here, however, genuine loving-kindness means wanting happiness and the cause of happiness for all sentient beings whether they are our friends or our enemies, and whether they are known to us or not known to us. One must generate this extensive loving-kindness by practice. The little loving-kindness that we naturally have is very important because it is the seed. With practice, we can grow this little loving-kindness into universal loving-kindness.

> **Compassion is the wish that others may be free from suffering and the cause of suffering, whether in saṃsāra, on the lesser vehicle, or in their resultant states.**

When you have developed loving-kindness, when you want every sentient being to possess happiness and the causes of happiness, you look around and you see that they are not happy. The nature of saṃsāra is suffering, just as the nature of fire is hot. Generally, no one is free from the four major sufferings: the suffering of birth, old age, sickness, and death. Moreover, in our lives, we encounter enemies, separation from loved ones, unwanted occurrences, and the inability to fulfill our hopes and desires. As human beings, we experience family problems, legal problems, relationship problems, financial problems—so many kinds of problems. No matter where you go or with whom you associate, there is no final satisfaction; there will always be something wrong or another reason to complain.

Compassion is the sincere wish that sentient beings who are suffering be free from suffering. All sentient beings in saṃsāra are experiencing suffering, so therefore you must wish that all sentient beings be free from suffering and the cause of suffering. To wish only for their freedom from suffering is insufficient because unless they are also free from the causes of suffering, they will suffer again.

Beings who are advanced on the lower yānas do not have ordinary sentient beings' visible sufferings, but they are also objects of compassion. Understand that there are two extremes. On one hand, there is saṃsāra, where one does not have any choice and is without any freedom. In saṃsāra, wherever the winds of karma and the defilements blow, one has no choice but to be blown there. There is great suffering in saṃsāra.

On the other hand, there is nirvāṇa, which is totally free from suffering. However, nirvāṇa is an inactive state, and it does not develop one's complete good qualities. With one's full qualities undeveloped, it is not possible to benefit others. Being in nirvāṇa is the biggest obstacle to attaining enlightenment. Once you are in there, it will take you many, many eons to attain enlightenment. Building a house is easier if you build it from the foundation up and do not need to reorganize a structure that has already been built. It is much easier to make changes to the plans than it is to change an existing house. Thus beings in nirvāṇa are also objects of compassion. They have not developed their full qualities, and attaining nirvāṇa is the greatest obstacle to attaining what we call non-abiding nirvāṇa, or the great nirvāṇa, which is above both saṃsāra and nirvāṇa.

> **Therefore always practice loving-kindness and compassion in this manner. If one has the thought of loving-kindness and compassion but hasn't engaged with skillful means, or if one has engaged but is not resolute, then these are still not for the purpose of others.**

Without loving-kindness and compassion you cannot generate enlightenment mind. In fact, compassion is the life force of all virtuous qualities. Lacking compassion is like having a body without life. On the other hand, possessing loving-kindness and compassion without skillful means is not of benefit to others.

A disabled mother who sees her child thrown into the water would be terrified and greatly wish to save her child, but because she is disabled she would be unable to help. Even though we might have loving-kindness and compassion, at the moment we cannot do very much to benefit beings because we are ordinary beings. We do not have the full knowledge, compassion, and power of enlightened beings. The only way to effectively help sentient beings is to attain buddhahood. Thus it says in the next verse:

> **Thus the perfect Buddha is the fruition of perfect wisdom, compassion, and supreme power that eradicates all faults and has perfected all good qualities.**

We must attain enlightenment. We might think that, although it would be a great thing to attain this, we are merely ordinary people. We might not have the courage or the willpower and think "How can we, ordinary sentient beings, attain buddhahood?" To encourage us, he writes:

> **His attainment was also dependent on sentient beings, therefore aspire that you shall do likewise. This is wishing enlightenment mind.**

The buddhas were once sentient beings. In the beginning they were ordinary beings who created enlightenment mind and subsequently attained enlightenment. We, like them, have buddha nature. We also have the skillful methods of the teachings. We possess the causes and the conditions, and there is no reason why we cannot succeed. You should not be discouraged, and you must have a strong aspiration. If, in order to save all sentient beings from the suffering of saṃsāra, you wish to attain enlightenment, this is called wishing enlightenment mind.

> **With this thought, under the auspices of a spiritual master, take the vow in accordance with the formal ritual. This is wishing enlightenment mind.**

If this great wish is made as a vow in a ritual before a spiritual preceptor, it is called creating wishing enlightenment mind.

> **Entering enlightenment mind is the intention to practice all the methods that accomplish buddhahood. Generating the resolution to do this is entering enlightenment mind.**

When you generate wishing enlightenment mind, you make the great aspiration to attain full enlightenment. But you must also aspire to engage in or enter the vast conduct of the bodhisattvas. This thought is called entering enlightenment mind. If you make this thought in the form of a vow in front of a preceptor, it is called creating entering enlightenment mind.

As this is a method to generate that which is not generated and to increase that which has been generated, aspire to it with great joy and perfect entering enlightenment mind through practice.

This entering enlightenment mind is a great way to generate bodhicitta in those in whom it has not been created. In those in whom it has already been created, it will increase. There are two kinds of bodhicitta, or enlightenment mind: relative and absolute. Relative enlightenment mind also has two parts: wishing and entering enlightenment mind.

A certain bodhisattva made the analogy that wishing enlightenment mind is like the wish to go, and entering enlightenment mind is like the actual act of going. Therefore reflect on methods of practicing the wishing and entering thoughts.

Wishing enlightenment mind can be compared to the wish to go to another country. Entering enlightenment mind is like actually setting out on the journey—packing your bags and traveling on the road until you reach your destination. Entering enlightenment mind is practicing in order to attain enlightenment, so one must practice diligently.

Only a handful can tell the various ways of differentiating between the mind and the enlightenment mind, and also between the wishing and the entering enlightenment mind, differentiated by practice. This is the relative enlightenment mind.

I think that the word *mind* here means wishing enlightenment mind rather than ordinary mind. There are three stages: the wishing enlightenment mind, the creation of the wishing enlightenment mind, and the keeping of the wishing enlightenment mind. Without the ritual, if when you hear of the great qualities of the Buddha and the great benefit of attaining enlightenment, you wish to attain enlightenment for the sake of all sentient beings, this is wishing enlightenment mind. If you make this mind as a vow in front of a preceptor before all the buddhas, saying, "I must attain ultimate enlightenment," then this is called the creation of enlightenment mind. It means that you have made this as a vow called the bodhisattva vow. After making the vow, you have to keep certain rules. You must not do things that go against the vow, and you must do things that are conducive to keeping the vow. These are the practices for keeping enlightenment mind. These are the three stages, and they are similar to entering enlightenment mind, creating the entering enlightenment mind, and keeping the entering enlightenment mind.

> **If examined, an entity is not unitary as it is interconnected. In the absence of the unitary, where is the multiplicity? What else could exist other than these two? Since there is no existence there is also no nonexistence. As these two contradict, neither is there both. As there is no basis of reason, neither is there not-both. Therefore under careful analysis, nothing can really exist. Even the mind also does not grasp at the sign. This is the cause that is similar to the ultimate enlightenment mind. This is also the view that is the supreme among all.**

This is an explanation of the absolute enlightenment mind, or the wisdom aspect. The relative enlightenment mind is the method aspect. Birds, in order to fly in the sky, need two wings, and similarly, in order to attain enlightenment, you need both method and wisdom. Method is like the legs and feet that enable you to walk on the road, and wisdom is like your eyes. If you have legs but no eyes, or eyes but no legs, then your journey will be impossible. The enlightenment mind that we have been talking about so far—wishing, entering, and the importance of practicing them—are all on the method side. The method aspect must be combined with the wisdom aspect, which is the absolute enlightenment mind.

The absolute enlightenment mind is the true nature of all phenomena. Reality and what we see as reality are two different things. Think of a person with a visual defect who sees a double image of the moon. This person sees two moons, but that is not reality. We are like this person; what we see and what we feel are not reality.

If you examine carefully, there is no entity that is just one. Everything is many. Take this table, for example. In our minds, we think of a table as one or as a unitary entity, but it is not. It is a collection of many pieces of wood joined together. If we see all these pieces of wood, we realize that "it" is many and where is this entity called "table"? And then each piece of wood can also be broken down or dismantled into many. Each is composed of smaller and smaller units, until we reach atoms. Imagine the smallest possible unit, so small that it cannot be divided any further. We might think that this tiny particle, this tiny atom, is one. But then even that atom, if it exists in space, must have sides facing the various directions, and therefore it again must be divisible. In this way, you cannot find any entity at all that is just one.

Next, when through analysis you cannot find one, how can you find many? How can you reach two, three, or many when you cannot even establish one? Yet how else can things exist other than as one and many?

Existence and nonexistence depend upon each other in the same way as "right" and "left." If there is no existence, you cannot have nonexistence. To speak of nonexistence implies that something existed before, or could exist but now does not. It assumes existence. Next, we cannot say that things both exist and don't exist, nor can we assert neither existence nor nonexistence. Reality—ultimate reality—is away from all extremes: the extremes of existence, nonexistence, both, and neither. It is beyond explanation, beyond perception, and beyond words. It is beyond perception because our mind is relative and relative mind cannot perceive the absolute.

This is the highest view. There are many different schools and philosophies other than Buddhism, and within Buddhism there are many different philosophical views. All of them, no matter what view they describe, fall into one of the two categories or the two extremes of eternalism or nihilism. Only what we call the Madhyamaka, or the middle way between these two extremes, is able to describe ultimate truth or reality.

The Buddha gave these teachings in the perfection of wisdom sūtras, which were later explained by the great master Nāgārjuna. The Buddha himself gave a prophecy that there would be a bhikṣu named Nāgārjuna who would be able to explain the ultimate and supreme view among all views.

> **Familiarize yourself with this ultimate enlightenment mind after ascertaining it through analogies, through reasoning, and by remaining in meditative equipoise without any grasping.**

Once you have cultivated the wisdom aspect, the method aspect becomes much more powerful. Through this one is able to accomplish enlightenment.

> **Knowing the shortcomings of saṃsāra and nirvāṇa, do not aspire for them. Through recollecting the qualities of the Buddha, always aspire for them.**

By knowing both the faults of saṃsāra and the faults of nirvāṇa, one will not have any desire for either of them. By remembering the great qualities of the Buddha, one will always have a strong aspiration to win buddhahood.

> **Feel joy in fulfilling the purpose of others through equalizing and exchanging oneself with others. This is the greatest skillful means to perfect the wishing enlightenment mind. Entering enlightenment mind is perfected through the accumulation of merit and wisdom. Practice it without discouragement or disappointment.**

At the moment we feel a vast difference between self and other. We continuously think of ourselves as primary and others as secondary. The first step in perfecting enlightenment mind is to make them equal. Just as one's own self is important to one, so it is with every sentient being. They all feel the same way, and they all long for happiness and to be free from suffering. You must learn to make yourself and others equal in importance.

After you are well-versed in this, you must practice exchanging self and other. In order to win enlightenment, you need to cut the root of saṃsāra, and the root of saṃsāra is self-clinging. Self-clinging is the source of all misery and all suffering, and the most effective way to eradicate it is to practice exchange meditation. To practice this, think that you are giving to others all joy and happiness, everything that is good, and think that you are taking from them all their misery, suffering, and pain. With this, one can destroy self-clinging. Practicing without any discouragement or disappointment is the way that all buddhas of the past, present, and future attain enlightenment. We who want to attain enlightenment must do like they did.

Entering enlightenment mind means to enter the bodhisattva path, and the main practice of the bodhisattva path is the accumulation of the two heaps of merit and wisdom. Doing this, you complete or accomplish entering enlightenment mind. The next verse explains this in more detail:

> **Perfect the Buddha's path by compassionately practicing all the six perfections without conceptualizing the three spheres and without procrastination or satiation. Fulfill completely all hopes of "those beings who are to be tamed by you" and place them on the stage of buddhahood. Endow all other sentient beings likewise.**

The bodhisattva's main or general practice is to practice the six perfections without conceptualizing the three spheres in order to gain the qualities of the Buddha from great compassion. The "three spheres" are the object, the subject, and the act. For example, when you practice generosity, the object is the recipient, the subject is you the giver, and the deed includes the gift.

Understand that in reality the three spheres have no inherent existence. They appear at the relative level. In reality there are no sentient beings, there is no self who is giving, and there is no deed or thing given. Only when practiced with this kind of wisdom does it become the pāramitā, or the perfection of generosity.

If giving is done with clinging to the ordinary mind of separateness of self, other, and thing, it will still be an act of generosity, but it will not be the pāramitā of generosity. The perfection of generosity means that the giving is done with the motivation of enlightenment mind, and that it is done with the wisdom of not conceptualizing the three spheres. This is when it becomes the perfection of generosity rather than just generosity. Wisdom is very important. The other perfections are like blind people, and wisdom is like the person with good eyes who leads them. When done with the wisdom that is devoid of the three spheres, an act of generosity, patience, or whatever becomes an actual cause of enlightenment. Otherwise, although it might be a virtuous deed, it is not a direct cause of enlightenment.

Also, you should not delay. You might be almost ready to give, and then you might think, "No, I will not give today. I will give tomorrow." This is not right because this thought is the exact opposite of generosity. You may also think, "Today I gave this much, and it is enough." In these ways, you might cling to the thought of not giving or to the thought that you have given enough. All the perfections—generosity, moral conduct, patience, effort, concentration, and wisdom—must be practiced in the way described here.

> **The perfection of generosity has the intention of giving everything—material things, protection, Dharma, and loving-kindness.**

There are four kinds of giving—material gifts, the gift of fearlessness, the gift of Dharma, and the gift of love.

> **The perfection of moral conduct has the intention to be free from any failing, to abandon faults, to accomplish merits, and to strive for the purpose of others.**

Moral conduct is acting without defilements by abstaining from negative deeds such as killing and stealing, and by performing virtuous deeds. Again, with all the perfections it is important to have the motivation of the enlightenment mind combined with the wisdom that is devoid of the three spheres. This is when moral conduct becomes the perfection of moral conduct.

> **The perfection of patience has the intention to be free from anger, to not cause trouble, and to ignore any harassment, and it is convinced that the Dharma is beneficial.**

The perfection of patience is a real, direct antidote to anger. Among the defilements, there is none more severe than anger. A single strong moment of anger can destroy the merits collected over a period of thousands of eons. Anger is the worst of all the defilements. If someone kills a living being in anger, then most probably that person will go to the hell realm. If, however, you kill a living being from desire—for the sake of wealth or to acquire the animal's flesh or skin—then it is said that you will go to the hungry ghost realm. If you kill an animal or any living being out of ignorance, not knowing that it is a negative deed—for example, with the idea that by sacrificing animals you can please the deities—then you will most probably go to the animal realm. Anger is a difficult thing, and the worst of the defilements. The one advantage is that anger is relatively easy to control. When we become angry, we are not happy, and this makes it easier to eliminate anger. Desire, for instance, may be less severe, but it is more difficult to eliminate. With desire comes good feelings and an idea of happiness. We cling to these, and so it is more difficult to give up desire.

> **The perfection of effort has the joyful intention to gather merits through armoring, practicing, not being discouraged, and being unrelenting**

Effort is having a great interest in practicing and being eager to practice virtuous deeds. Having effort is like wearing armor and becoming strong.

> **The perfection of concentration has the intention to not let the mind waver by turning the mind inward and away from all external objects and by placing the mind totally on mind itself.**

Normally the mind is always wavering. It is always in motion like a stream of thoughts. With this continual stream of thoughts, one cannot achieve inner meditative stabilization. Therefore one must sit and practice concentration. By recognizing the five faults, by applying the eight antidotes, and through the nine methods, one should attain meditative concentration.

In the beginning, we practice with an outer object. Later, the focus is mind itself. Eventually one's mind will be able to remain in single-pointed concentration without the interference of thoughts. It will be steady, clear, and bright, like a candle without any disturbance from the wind. This is called calm-abiding concentration, or meditation.

> **The perfection of wisdom has the intention to know all by analyzing after comprehending the relative truth and by realizing that nature which is free of inherent existence.**

One wants to know the truth of things. Ordinary people do not bother much to wonder about this, but more intelligent people try find out about the nature of reality. And so people have analyzed, investigated, and employed sharp reasoning and logical thought, and they have come to different conclusions. There are many different schools, non-Buddhist and Buddhist, all of them with different philosophical views about the nature of reality.

After carefully analyzing relative truth—the things that we see and feel—we realize that there is no inherent existence. Everything depends upon causes and conditions. When causes and conditions come together in a certain way, certain things appear. When any of the necessary causes or conditions is missing, that thing will disappear. This is like a dream. Because we fall asleep, because of the propensities of our daytime life, and so on, we see our dreams. In our dreams, we see so many different things, and while we are dreaming our experiences are as real as this life. Dreams can give you joy. Dreams can give you pleasure. Dreams can give you worry. Dreams can make you frightened. Dreams can make you sad and they can make you cry. The experiences seem as real as this life. Yet the moment you wake up, there is nothing there. Everything is gone, and there is not even the slightest sign of what you saw in your dream. This life is like that. The only difference is that what we experience now in this life has more stable propensities, and these make it more difficult to realize it as unreal.

In reality, all phenomena are devoid of inherent existence. This is what we mean by wisdom. This is why it applies to the other pāramitās, as when we practice generosity devoid of the three spheres; there is no inherent existence in the giver, in the recipient, or in the gift. Although there appears to be these three things, in reality the three spheres of object, subject, and act are devoid of inherent existence. If you practice giving with this wisdom, then it becomes the perfection of wisdom. It is the same with moral conduct, patience, effort, and concentration. Wisdom is very important.

> **Gradually all faults such as miserliness, immoral conduct, anger, laziness, distraction, and ignorance are destroyed, as the six perfections act as their antidotes.**

Generosity acts as an antidote to miserliness. The antidote to immoral conduct is moral conduct. The antidote to anger is patience. The antidote to laziness is effort. The antidote to distraction is concentration. The antidote to ignorance is wisdom.

> **Prosperity, birth in higher realms, pleasant physical features, fulfillment of aspirations, peace of mind, and being learned among all the wise are the temporary results.**

This verse describes the temporary results of practicing the perfections. By practicing generosity, you gain prosperity. By practicing moral conduct, you will take birth in the higher realms. By practicing patience, you will have pleasant physical features. By practicing effort, all your wishes will be fulfilled. Practicing concentration will bring peace of mind. Practicing wisdom will make you learned among the wise. These are the temporary or worldly results, and they will be acquired in addition to the ultimate result. We all wish for things such as prosperity and to be born into the higher realms. While prayer and aspiration have power, they are not enough to fulfill these wishes. But through our practice of Dharma—for example, by practicing generosity—we are sure to gain prosperity.

> **The first five perfections continuously increase the accumulation of merit. The sixth fully completes the accumulation of wisdom.**

The first five perfections—generosity, moral conduct, and so on—complete the merit heap. The sixth perfection of wisdom completes the wisdom heap.

> **In addition, the fifth is śamatha and the sixth is vipaśyanā. It is said that with an analytical mind that abides in calm, all remaining meanings can be grasped.**

Śamatha is concentration or calm-abiding meditation. At the moment our minds are very busy, and we experience a stream of thoughts arising one after another. Through concentration practice the mind becomes calm. It is not easy. Yet if one practices regularly, calm abiding can be achieved. It is like exercising the body. Doing it once may not bring any apparent change, but if you do it regularly there will definitely be improvement.

This concentration, I think, is very difficult for ordinary people because we are just not used to it. We are used to the stream of thoughts, so it is very difficult to sit and remain still and set the mind in single-pointedness. However, if you do it regularly—it will take time, and you should not be discouraged—I am sure that you will improve and become able to remain in complete calm.

On the basis of that calm, next one does vipaśyanā meditation, which means to have insight or to see something that you did not see before. Ordinarily we do not see ultimate reality; we cannot access it. We can only have some ideas about it from texts and from explanations, but we do not have an actual experience or vision of it. But through meditation, the meaning of this becomes more stable, more definite.

> **The former pacifies negative emotions and renders clear concentration and also clairvoyance. The latter eradicates all faults and completely perfects wisdom and primordial wisdom.**

Calm-abiding meditation calms the defilements. Through calm-abiding meditation, even very strong anger or very strong desire can be pacified. It also establishes a base for meditation, and it will cause clairvoyance to arise. This arises naturally when your mind becomes more clear and more subtle. For example, while we are dreaming our minds are much more subtle.

Then, through the practice of vipaśyanā, or insight wisdom, the defilements are removed entirely. The method aspect—loving-kindness, compassion, and enlightenment mind—suppresses the defilements and makes them inactive so that anger and desire, for example, do not arise. The roots of these defilements, however, are still present. Vipaśyanā digs out the roots of the defilements so that they are completely destroyed and so that it becomes impossible for anger or desire to arise.

> **Moral conduct is the foundation of both calm abiding and wisdom. The remaining three are the conducive conditions for their accomplishment. If well analyzed, each perfection embodies the six perfections together with śamatha and vipaśyanā. Therefore realizing that each of them embodies the six and the two, constantly practice and familiarize. Buddhahood is then not far.**

Good moral conduct is the foundation for all good qualities. To build a tall building you need a firm foundation; likewise for all the other practices, good moral conduct is very important. When you keep good discipline, your mind is clear. When your mind is clear, your practice is better. Good moral conduct is the base for both śamatha and vipaśyanā, while generosity, patience, and effort count as conducive conditions. However, if we analyze them carefully, each practice contains all the six together. For example, in the practice of generosity, while we are giving we are also abstaining from negative deeds. While we are giving, we are also practicing patience and effort. We are also concentrating upon what we are doing, and we are also doing it with the wisdom that is devoid of the three spheres.

In the beginning we are not accustomed to the practices. We are not accustomed to patience, for example, so when someone says something very nasty to us it is very difficult to be patient. If, however, you have done it once today for the very first time, then you should be able do it two times tomorrow—and do it a little more easily. Then you can do it three times the day after that. If you proceed gradually in this way, you will grow used to it. And for the person doing this, buddhahood is not far. Buddhahood is very, very near!

The four means of amassing disciples ripen sentient beings. Material gifts beckon all beings who are to be tamed and place them in temporary happiness. Pleasant speech correctly teaches the six perfections. Then guide them in right behavior, and cause them to be joyful because one's own actions are according to the meaning.

The six perfections are for self-ripening and to make ourselves into bodhisattvas. The four means of amassing disciples are different. Both include the practice of giving, but in the four means of amassing disciples, the practice of generosity is for gathering or calling disciples to the path. The other three means are speaking pleasantly, leading through skillful means, and, in order to provide encouragement, practicing very diligently yourself.

The first amasses disciples through material gifts and the remaining three through Dharma. The former benefits and the latter liberates. The purpose of others is completely included within these.

The means of giving material gifts is in order to benefit people, and the remaining three of the means comprise the explanation and practice of Dharma.

Gathering the two accumulations and putting effort into the two purposes should be carried out with the thought that everything is like an illusion. Familiarization in the practice without any conceptualization is the method of noble beings. Attempt to directly perceive enlightenment, which is like the nature of the sky, with a mind that is free of obscurations.

The two accumulations are the merit heap and the wisdom heap, and the two purposes are fulfilling one's own purpose and fulfilling the purpose of others. When you perform these practices with the thought that everything is like an illusion or a magical show, and if you practice nonconceptualization, then, as you proceed, your obscurations will grow smaller and smaller and you will become closer and closer to reality.

> **Merit and wisdom are the two wheels of a chariot. Skillful means is the wooden shaft, and vast vows are the supporting elements. The supreme horse endowed with the limbs of mindfulness, enthusiasm, and deep concentration gradually assembles one, two, three charioteers of aspiration and so forth, and enters into the path to liberation. This is called the path of accumulation.**

The path of accumulation, the first of the five paths, has three levels: the small, medium, and great. The example is a chariot with two wheels pulled by a horse. The means of moving forward, the strong limbs of the horse, are mindfulness, enthusiasm or diligence, and concentration.

> **Riding such a great chariot, you will gradually be endowed with the limbs of the five spiritual faculties and the limbs of the five powers. Fastening one and two elephants, enter into the well-differentiated path and reach the huge ocean of the wisdom of exalted beings. This is called the path of application.**

The path of application, the second of the five paths, is the joint between the worldly level and the beyond-worldly level. This path has four levels: the "heat," the "tip," "patience," and "excellent Dharma." When day breaks at dawn, before you can see the sun, you can see the light of the sun. The path of application is like this. Realization becomes brighter and clearer as you approach the beyond-worldly level.

> **Completely eradicate all thick faults on the path of seeing while traveling the stages and the paths. Like the radiance of the sky is reflected on the surface of the ocean, maintain the mind in the one taste of meditative equipoise and the dharmadhātu. The supreme shore of the ocean of primordial wisdom of the**

precious seven limbs of enlightenment is seen for the first time. Traveling toward it after seeing it is called the path of seeing.

When you reach the path of seeing, you have reached the first bhūmi. All obscurations are cleared away. Your mind becomes like the reflection of the blue sky in the ocean. The meditative mind and ultimate reality are completely merged together; you see ultimate reality. From this point on the path and onward, you are really the same as the Buddha; the difference is one of degree or fullness rather than kind, like the difference between the new moon and the full moon. When you attain the path of seeing, you are totally free of the defilements and the suffering of birth, old age, sickness, and death. You have eradicated all forms of obscurations that are the defilements, and you are eliminating obscurations to knowledge.

The huge ship of nonconceptual wisdom adorned with the eight limbs of the banners of the noble path of enlightenment travels toward the shore of the peaceful dharmadhātu, blown by the constant and harmonious winds of the blessing of the Buddha. In the process, the ocean tides, which are like the faults to be abandoned through meditation, are all abandoned, and the bodhisattvas-in-training gain control over the precious Dharma of exalted beings. Familiarization through meditation with the meaning that was previously seen is the path of meditation.

Some category systems describe ten bhūmis, but according to the Mahāyāna, there are eleven. The first bhūmi is called the path of seeing. The next nine, from the second bhūmi to the tenth, are called the path of meditation, during which your meditation increases like the moon. The eleventh bhūmi, according to the Pāramitāyāna, is buddhahood or ultimate enlightenment.

In this way, crossing land and sea, just as you traversed the mundane and supramundane paths, enter the port of the island of the wish-fulfilling jewel. Now your voyage is complete; all

unfavorable conditions are destroyed; all good qualities are perfected. Thus this path is called the path of perfection.

Obscurations to knowledge are gross, medium, and fine; as you go forward, increasingly fine and subtle obscurations are eliminated. On the nine stages, only very subtle obscurations to knowledge remain. When the fine obscurations are eliminated, you have reached the path of no-more-learning, which is the ultimate goal.

The supramundane path is also categorized in ten stages. Like ocean water is the same but appears differently depending upon the base, so the process of liberation is the same but categorized according to bases and qualities.

The realization is the same even though it continues to grow, just like the moon on the first day of its waxing is the same moon as the full moon. *Bhūmi* means earth, and just as the earth is the base for all things animate and inanimate, the bhūmis are the base for all the qualities.

The stages are so called because each produces its qualities and acts as support for innumerable beings.

"Great Joy" is so called because it enters the stage nearing buddhahood and takes joy in generosity.

"Stainless" is so called because it is free from the stains of immoral conduct or broken moral conduct.

The first bhūmi is called "Great Joy." It is the same as the path of seeing. When you reach the second bhūmi, even your dreams are free from immorality, so it is called "Stainless."

"Luminous" is so called because it is endowed with the light of the Dharma of scripture and the radiance of patience.

The bhūmis are associated with the perfections. "Great Joy" is associated with generosity, and "Stainless" is associated with moral conduct. Here, "Luminous" is said to be endowed with the radiance of patience.

> **"Radiant" is so called because the fire that burns the faults of conceptual phenomena is ablaze with enthusiasm.**

> **"Extremely Difficult to Conquer" is so called because it purifies those that are difficult to purify and guards the mind through concentration.**

This bhūmi is called "Extremely Difficult to Conquer" because conceptual thoughts are so difficult to control. This bhūmi is associated with the fifth perfection, the perfection of concentration or meditation.

> **"Approaching" is so called because all the phenomena of saṃsāra and nirvāṇa are perceived directly through reliance on wisdom.**

This completes the six pāramitās, and the first six bhūmis. Sometimes, however, ten pāramitās are referred to. The additional four are skillful means, aspiration, spiritual power, and primordial wisdom.

> **"Gone Far" is so called because it distances from the signs and excels through supreme skillful means.**

"Gone Far" means even the most subtle of the obscurations of phenomena are removed.

> **"Immovable" is so called because it is not shaken by any conceptual thought and firmly abides in aspiration.**

> **"Good Intelligence" is so called because it teaches the Dharma through four pure thoughts and great power.**

This is the perfection of power.

> **The "Dharma Cloud" is so called as the cloud of concentration and mantras gather in the sky of primordial wisdom.**

This completes the ten bhūmis related to the accomplishment of the ten perfections, each with its own distinctive qualities.

> **Thereafter, through vajra-like samādhi, the door to the precious treasure opens. Then this power transforms these four and buddhahood is attained, which is a treasure of immeasurable qualities and the only teacher or relative of all sentient beings.**

These are the different stages of the bodhisattva path. After the ten bhūmis, you reach the eleventh bhūmi, which, according to the Mahāyāna path, is ultimate enlightenment.

> **Like clouds that disappear in the sky, the stains that are the obscurations disappear, and the dharmadhātu and primordial wisdom converge into one taste. This is called the natural body, the svābhāvikakāya.**

When the obscurations of the defilements and the obscurations to knowledge, including their propensities, disappear like clouds dissolving in the sky, then the dharmadhātu, or the true nature of our mind, free from all forms of obscurations, is manifested. Then it is merged with ultimate reality, called the *dharmatā*. This is the svābhāvikakāya.

> **Due to the power of immeasurable skillful means and compassion, great bliss and the five certainties of the pure realm, teacher, disciple, time, and Dharma are enjoyed. This is called the enjoyment body, the saṃbhogakāya.**

Where does the dharmakāya come from? There is, in fact, no change from before. It is simply manifested. It is a matter of just seeing it. The dharmakāya is not something that you acquire from outside yourself; it is not something that you newly acquire. It is something that we all have right from the beginning. At the moment we do not see it due to obscurations, but once the obscurations are cleared, the dharmakāya is there spontaneously.

The good qualities, however, *are* newly gained. The saṃbhogakāya has the five certainties. The first is the certainty of place: the saṃbhogakāya does not reside in any place other than the highest buddha realm, known as Akaniṣṭha.

Second, its form is the form of the great teacher, the Buddha, the highest physical body. Our ordinary physical body is transformed into a buddha's body possessing the thiry-two signs and the eighty qualities. Our ordinary voice is transformed into the melodies of Brahmā with sixty branches. Our ordinary mind is transformed into omniscient transcendental wisdom.

Next are the disciples. The saṃbhogakāya does not have ordinary disciples, only bodhisattvas who have reached the irreversible state.

Finally, the saṃbhogakāya only teaches the highest Mahāyāna teachings.

In the saṃbhogakāya there is the enjoyment of complete bliss, and this why it is called saṃbhogakāya, which means "enjoyment body." The dharmakāya is the result gained for one's own purpose, and all the qualities of the saṃbhogakāya are for the sake of other beings. There are some scholars who say that all the qualities of the saṃbhogakāya—dwelling in a celestial palace, having the physical body of a buddha—are appearances for the sake of other beings and that a buddha himself does not see these, instead dwelling in the highest possible state. But other scholars say that a buddha also sees them.

> **The powers of knowing the right and wrong place, action, faculty, element, inclination, path of all goals, placing on liberation, recollection of places of past lives, recollection of birth and death, and eradication of defilements. These are the ten powers of the muni, the Lord Buddha, because like a vajra he removes all obscurations, the hordes of demons, and other opponents.**

There are unique qualities of the Buddha that are not possessed by other noble beings. Among these unique qualities are the ten powers that are enumerated here. These are unique powers possessed by fully enlightened beings to remove obscurations and defeat obstacles.

The next set of qualities that are unique to a buddha is the four fearlessnesses:

> **The Buddha has no qualms about teaching perfectly and accurately on relinquishment, primordial wisdom, the path of renunciation, and impediments. These are therefore the four fearlessnesses, because like a powerful lion he defeats opponents and prevails over disciples or beings who are to be tamed.**

The Buddha experiences no obstructions. For example, śrāvakas and pratyekabuddhas possess clairvoyance, but they are not able to know everything. Their clairvoyance is limited by distance and by limits of time.

Once there was a devotee whom the arhats examined, wondering whether he possessed the seed of liberation or not. But the Buddha was able to say immediately, "Yes, he has the seed." The Buddha explained that a long time ago he was born as a pig. That pig was chased by a dog. It so happened that the pig and the dog circled clockwise around a stūpa, and in this way the seed was planted. The Buddha was able to answer this straight away, while the arhats did not know. The Buddha can answer anything, no matter how far into the past or how distant in the future, and no matter how far away in space. He has absolutely no obstructions, and therefore he possesses fearlessness.

It also happened that at one time there were seven worms upon a leaf. The leaf was floating on a lake, and in the middle of the lake was a statue of Buddha Vairocana. It so happened that the wind blew this little leaf so that it went clockwise around the statue. Of course, this happened accidentally. However, due to this merit, these worms were born as humans and they married seven daughters of a father who was an untouchable. Because they were untouchables, of course, they were treated very badly. These men received wages for cutting grass, and they offered money from their wages to monks. Because of this merit, in their next lives they were born as seven princes of a royal family. They met a spiritual master and created the enlightenment mind. Later, they all became bodhisattvas and attained enlightenment.

One should not neglect even the tiniest of virtuous deeds. Even though those worms and that pig were not able to know what they were doing, they did those things and the results were obtained. We as human beings have knowledge. So if we do a lot of prostrations, there is great merit!

> **Free from erroneous speech and idle chatter; free from heedlessness and remaining in meditative equipoise; abandoning discriminating thoughts; having nonanalytical equanimity; without weakened aspiration, perseverance, mindfulness, or wisdom; and without weakened liberation and primordial wisdom, the physical, verbal, and mental actions are coupled with wisdom. Primordial wisdom knows the past, future, and present without obstruction. These are the eighteen distinguished qualities of the enlightened one, which are like the sky that pervades all yet is unstained by any. This is the quality of relinquishment. The good qualities are countless if categorized.**

These are the special distinguishing qualities of a buddha. A buddha, for example, remains in meditative equipoise. Arhats and others, while they perform meditation, remain very mindful and engaged in careful examination, but while off session they may not be mindful or may be distracted. A buddha is not like this.

This passage enumerates eighteen unique or distinguishing qualities of buddhas, but actually there is no limit to their good qualities. Birds fly through the sky and eventually tire and come back to the ground. They do not stop because they have run out of space in which to fly. Space is endless, but their strength is limited and so they must stop. Likewise, no one is able to fully describe the Buddha's qualities because anyone's ability would be exhausted. For example, those who have gained the power of speech are able to go on describing the qualities of buddhas for eons, but such an enumeration would not decrease the totality of those qualities at all. They are immeasurable.

Understand that the ten faculties that are mentioned elsewhere are included within this.

These are the qualities gained after relinquishing all obscurations. When the obscurations are cleared, you will gain these great and unique qualities of a buddha.

The body is endowed with thirty-two marks of the ripened result for the purpose of others.

As I said before, the physical bodies of buddhas are mainly for the sake of other beings. A buddha's body is created out of great merits, so even just the sight of a buddha's body has great benefit.

Many people have asked questions about who can see the Buddha. Can ordinary people see the Buddha? If not, then what stage of attainment is necessary in order to see the Buddha? These questions were raised when Chögyal Phagpa was traveling to China. He responded that there are two ways of seeing the Buddha. One way is through one's own power, and the other way is through the power of others. Through the power of others an ordinary person can see the Buddha. However, it is necessary to reach at least the path of accumulation in order to see the Buddha by one's own power.

This means that if the Buddha happened to come here, for example, then we who are residing in this area would be able to see him not because of our own power but because of the power of others: for example, because of the power of those who invited him here. Seeing the Buddha by one's own power means that even if the Buddha were not invited here, by your own merit you would still be able to see the Buddha in your pure vision.

The feet are even and marked by wheels. Heels are broad and the toes are long. The toes are webbed with feet smooth and tender. The seven features of the body are prominent and the ankles are like those of an antelope. The private organ is concealed in a sheath and the upper part of the body is like that of a lion. Shoulders are broad, and the points of the shoulders

are rounded. Hands are long and the supreme body is perfectly pure. The throat is stainless like a conch. Jaws are like that of a lion with forty teeth. The teeth are all the same size and evenly set, and the fangs are white. The tongue is long and endowed with excellent taste. The voice is like that of a kalaviṅka bird. The supreme eyes are deep blue in color with thick eyelashes. The precious hair is very white. The uṣṇīṣa is very high and cannot be seen even when peered at. The skin is thin and gold in color. The hairs grow to the right. The hair is the color of sapphire. The body has the proportion of a banyan tree. These are the thirty-two marks that excel those of powerful beings.

There once was a bodhisattva who set about traveling all the way to see the tip of the Buddha's uṣṇīṣa. He ascended very far, through many higher realms, and even then he could not see it. I have been told that it is not that tall, but still you can never see the tip, no matter how far you go.

A buddha's voice can be heard and will sound the same no matter how far away or near you are. You can hear a buddha everywhere, without the need for microphones! You can hear him in your own language as well. Whether you are a god, a nāga, a yakṣa, or a human, you will hear him speaking your language without simultaneous translation.

The size of a buddha is also much bigger or much taller than other beings. Perhaps you remember that in Kushinagar there is a statue of the reclining Buddha. I was told that this is the actual size of the Buddha's body, but I don't know.

The eighty minor marks are elaborations of these. This is the glory of the rūpakāya.

The eighty minor marks include having nails like copper, and so on. They elaborate the thirty-two major marks.

Just as the full moon shines brightly among the stars on a very clear autumn night, the Buddha shines amid the tenth-bhūmi bodhisattvas.

The Buddha dwells like a full moon in a sky of bright stars.

> **And just like children become happy when seeing reflections of the full moon in the water, a buddha's appearance accomplishes the purposes, and merit is consistently accumulated. This is explained by following the instructions of the Mahāyāna sūtras.**

Just like the reflection of the moon in water, those who have enough merit can see the Buddha.

> **Through the power of the saṃbhogakāya, in accordance with the merits of innumerable beings, the nirmāṇakāya appears in different forms and performs activities.**

Nirmāṇakāya means an "emanation body." This is very different from the saṃbhogakāya. The nirmāṇakāya can appear anywhere, even in this ordinary world. It also appears in whatever form is required—not necessarily in the form of a buddha. The nirmāṇakāya can appear as many things, as a śrāvaka, a universal emperor, a king or queen, a minister, an ordinary being, a monk or nun, or even as an animal. Also, while the saṃbhogakāya manifests no birth and no entering of mahāparinirvāṇa, the nirmāṇakāya does not remain forever.

> **The svābhāvikakāya embodies the supreme primordial wisdom of the dharmadhātu. The saṃbhogakāya is none other than mirror-like wisdom.**

The Buddha has five wisdoms, and the first, the wisdom of the dharmadhātu, is the dharmakāya. The second wisdom, mirror-like wisdom, is the saṃbhogakāya. The next two—the wisdom of equality and the wisdom of discrimination—are features of the saṃbhogakāya, as the next verse explains:

> **The wisdom of equality and the wisdom of discrimination**

are its features. The wisdom of accomplishment embodies the nirmāṇakāya.

The wisdom of accomplishment, the fifth wisdom, is the nirmāṇakāya.

All these bodies and primordial wisdoms are consecutively the containers and contained. The purpose of oneself and the purpose of others, the subtle and gross, are laid down similarly.

The Buddha's qualities are immeasurable, but they can be classified or categorized in many ways: as container and contained, for the purpose of oneself and for the purpose of others, as subtle and gross, and so on.

The Buddha is also ever unceasing: being the same flavor as the dharmadhātu, born out of an inexhaustible cause, destroying all unfavorable factors, fulfilling all aspirations, gaining power to overcome all, and because the objective of his activities is without end.

The dharmadhātu is unchanging and so too is the Buddha. His activities never cease, and this is because saṃsāra has no limit. If a million sentient beings were to attain enlightenment right now, the number of sentient beings remaining in saṃsāra would not decrease. The Buddha's activities will remain as long as saṃsāra remains.

Avalokiteśvara took a vow to remain in saṃsāra and not to attain enlightenment until all sentient beings have attained enlightenment. This is the highest kind of enlightenment and is known as having a "shepherd-like" enlightenment mind. A shepherd herds all his animals into safety first; he goes last. Of course, Avalokiteśvara, having made this enlightenment mind, had already attained enlightenment. This was his vow.

When Avalokiteśvara created enlightenment mind, he also made a kind of curse on himself: "If I give up this enlightenment mind," he vowed, "may my body be broken into a thousand pieces." And then for countless days and nights, for an incredibly long period of time, he rescued a great many beings from their suffering. He helped innumerable sentient beings to attain liberation. Finally, after a very long time, he looked at saṃsāra to see what kind of decrease there was in the number of suffering sentient beings. But there was no decrease; in fact, he saw that the number had increased. At this, Avalokiteśvara was very discouraged and thought, "How many beings have I saved? Yet now I see there is no end to the number of sentient beings, and I cannot help them all." With this, he gave up the thought of enlightenment and his body cracked into a thousand pieces.

His guru, Amitābha, appeared to him and said, "My son, what you have done is not right. You should take enlightenment mind again and generate an even larger enlightenment mind than before." Buddha Amitābha blessed the thousand pieces of his body, which became Avalokiteśvara with one thousand arms. His head, which was broken into ten pieces, became ten heads, and Buddha Amitābha set his own face on the top. Thus one-thousand-armed Avalokiteśvara has eleven faces, one thousand arms, and one thousand eyes.

> **His teachings will also continuously remain in this mundane world. There is no appearance and nonappearance, rising and settling, increasing and diminishing. It is taught that what is seen arises because of conceptual thought and the power of karma and not because of the condition of the locality.**

The Buddha's appearance or nonappearance, and so on, is due to our conceptual thoughts and our karma. It only seems that the Buddha's teachings are sometimes remaining in the world and at other times they will not remain. In reality, they are there all the time, like the sun, which is there all the time, even when we do not see it.

> **Likewise the sky and the sun are both seen to appear and to disappear, but in reality it is not actually so. Similarly, the Buddha continuously blesses pure yogis. Wonderful they are indeed, engaged always in the festival of the nectar of Dharma.**

For those who are pure yogis, the Buddha is always bestowing blessings, and they will always enjoy the nectar of the Dharma.

> **This is a brief oral teaching of the Mahāyāna tradition. For more, learn from others for the sake of the unsurpassable great purpose. This ends the third part, which explains the Mahāyāna tradition.**

Conclusion

> **If the Dharmic path for worldly beings is followed, then the god realms are not far. Further, if you climb the staircase of gods and humans, then liberation is very near.**

If you become a good human being and follow a virtuous life, then you will be born into the god realms in your future. When you take birth in a higher realm—in one of the god realms or as a human—then liberation is near. Although every being has the seed of buddhahood, human beings have the best chance for attaining enlightenment. This is why it says liberation is near.

> **It is said that all the results that are gained through the three yānas are the result of the one yāna. So I have explained here in accordance with the sequence of meaning.**

There are three yānas, and all of them lead eventually to the one yāna. When you are traveling a long distance, you cannot go all the way at once. You will find that there are places of rest. The other yānas offer temporary resting places, but eventually all will arrive upon the path to ultimate enlightenment.

> **In fact, the noble assembly, which has realized emptiness, and also the very learned have illuminated the teaching again and again in many different ways. Here I have explained briefly and**

concisely, as advice for you to consider and also for the benefit of others.

The Buddha's teaching has been explained before in many ways and by many great masters. This explanation, Chögyal Phagpa says, has been given in a short form and for the sake of the prince, as well as for the benefit of others.

May the wise forgive me for any mistakes in this text as my mind is like a child's. I haven't studied all knowledge extensively, and I have taught incoherently. By this merit, may all beings lead a proper worldly life and become buddhas by entering the door of Dharma.

This is the dedication.

***A Garland of Jewels*, a collection of advice to Prince Gibek Timur, was composed by Chögyal Phagpa at the great Sakya Monastery on the eighth day of the *guwu* month in the Male Fire Tiger Year. It contains two hundred and four stanzas.**

With this, we have completed the teaching.

Table of Tibetan Transliteration

Bande Shekyema	bande shed bskyed ma
bardo	bar do
Bönpo	bon po
bu	bu
chag	chak
Chak Lotsawa	Chag Lo tsa ba
chang	chang
ching sang	ching sangs
chö dung karpo	chos dung dkar po
Chöjé Ürgyen	Chos rje dbu rgyan
Chökyi Gönpo	Chos kyi mgon po
Chomden Raldri	Bcom ldan ral gri
Dampa chökyi chokha	Dam pa chos kyi phyogs kha
Darapa	mda ra pa
Do Kham Gang	mdo khams sgang
Doklowa Dulzin Shākya Jangchup	Mdog glo ba 'Dul 'dzin shākya byang chub
Drakpa Öser	Grags pa 'od zer
Drakpa Sengé	Grags pa seng ge
Drakpa Shönu	Grags pa gzhon nu
Drakphukpa Gewai Shenyen Bumpa Öser	Brag phug pa dge ba'i bshes gnyen 'Bum pa 'od zer
Drogön Chögyal Phagpa	'Gro mgon chos rgyal 'phags pa
Duchö Labrang	dus mchod bla brang
Dungrab Yarap Khagyen	*Gdung rabs ya rabs kha rgyan*
Epashang Ngönpawa Rinpoché Dorjé	E pa zhang mngon pa ba rin po che rdo rje

Gelong Kunlo	Dge slong kun blo
Geshé Drekhüpa	Dges bshes 'Bras khud pa
Gonagmi Chokha	Mgo nag mi'i phyogs kha
guwu	dgu bu
Gyatso	Brgya tsho
Gyeling Tai Chokha	Gyad gling rta'i phyogs kha
Gyerbuba Tsokgom Kungapal	Sgyer bu ba Tshogs sgom kun dga' dpal
Jamgön Ameshap Ngawang Kunga Sönam	'Jam mgon A myes zhabs Ngag dbang kun dga' bsod nams
Jang	Ljang
Jasa Böyikma	'Ja' sa bod yig ma
jenang	rjes gnang
Jetsun Dampa Kunga Drolchok	Rje btsun dam pa Kun dga' grol mchog
Jetsun Drakpa Gyaltsen	Rje btsun Grags pa rgyal mtshan
Jé Yangönpa	Rje Yang dgon pa
Jilbubai Geshé Taktön Sherab Óser	Rjil bu ba'i dge bshes Stag ston shes rab 'od zer
Joden	Jo gdan
Joden Jangpa Sönam Gyaltsen	Jo gdan byang pa bsod nams rgyal mtshan
Jowo	Jo bo
Kadampa	bka' gdams pa
Kamchuwa	Skam mchu ba
Kangyur	bka' 'gyur
Karma Pakshi	Karma pakshi
Kawa Paltsek	Ska ba dpal brtsegs
Kham	khams
khata	kha btags
Khön	'khon
Kunga Sangpo	Kun dga' bzang po
Kyidrong	Skyid grong
Kyormo lungpa	Skyor mo lung pa
Lama Tashi Pal	Bla ma Bkra shis dpal

Lamdré	lam 'bras
Langripa	Glang ri pa
Laruwa	La ru ba
Lhajé Darma Sengé	Lha rje Dar ma seng ge
Lhakang Chenmo	lha khang chen mo
Lhakang Labrang	lha khang bla brang
Lhasa Zongpa	Lha sa Rdzong pa
Lhochok palgyi ri	Lho phyogs dpal gyi ri
Lodrö Gyaltsen Palsangpo	Blo gros Rgyal mtshan dpal bzang po
Lotsawa Paltsek	Lo tsā ba Dpal brtsegs
Lowo Lotsāwa Sherab Rinchen	Glo bo Lo tsā ba Shes rab rin chen
lu	klu
Machig Kunkyi	Ma gcig kun skyid
Mahāsiddha Yöntenpal	Grub thob chen mo Yon tan dpal
Malo	Ma lo
Milarepa	Mi la res pa
Minyak	mi nyag
Mön	mon
Namkhabum	Nam mkha' 'bum
Nampharwa Tsulrin	Gnam phar ba tshul rin
Narthang	Snar thang
Narthang Abbot Chim Namkhadrak	Snar thang pa'i mkhan po Mchims nam mkha' grags
Ngamringi Lukhung	Ngam ring gi klu khung
Ngari	Mnga' ris
Ngönpawa Wangchuk Tsondrü	Mngon pa ba Dbang phyug brtson 'grus
Nyenchenpa	Nyan chen pa
Nyethang	Snye thang
Nyima Pal	Nyi ma dpal
Öserbum of Sala	Gsal la ba 'od zer 'bum
phagpa	'phags pa
Pomralha	Spom ra lha
Rangwen Marpa Naljor Wangchuk Galo	Rang dben Dmar pa rnal 'byor dbang phyug rgwa lo

riktsok	rigs tshogs
Rinchen Gang Labrang	Rin chen sgang Bla brang
ringsel	ring bsrel
Rinpoche Kyopapal	Rin po che Skyob pa dpal
Rongpa Khenpo Sengé Silnön	Rong pa mkhan po Seng ge zil gnon
Rong Rilung Phukpa	Rong Ri lung phug pa
Sachen Kunga Nyingpo	Sa chen Kun dga snying po
Sakya	Sa skya
Sakya Dungrab	*Sa skya'i gdung rabs*
Sakyapa	Sa skya pa
Sakyapa Ngawang Kunga Sönam	Sa skya pa Ngag dbang kun dga' bsod nams
sangtönpa	gsang ston pa
Sangtsa Sönam Gyaltsen	Zangs tsha bsod nams rgyal mtshan
Sangwanyen Ösung Gönpo	Gsang ba gnyan 'Od srungs mgon po
Satön Ripa	Sa ston ri pa
Serthok Chenmo	Gser thog chen mo
Shangdrü Monastery	Shang grud kyi dgon pa
Shang Gyalwa Pal	Zhang Rgyal ba dpal
Shang Könchok Pal	Zhang Dkon mchog dpal
Shang Lhabu	Shangs lha bu
Shangshungpa Dorjé Óser	Zhang zhung pa Rdo rje 'od zer
Sheldam Lingdrukma	Shel dam Gling drug ma
Sherab Sengé	Shes rab seng ge
shing	zhing
Sinshing	Zin shing
Sokla Kyapo	Sog la skya po
Sönam Tsemo	Bsod nams rtse mo
Songtsen Gampo	Srong btsan sgam po
Sulungpa	Sru lung pa
Surkhangi Gyatso	Zur khang gi Bgya tsho
tago	rta mgo
Takthog Shimocher	Stag thog gzhis mo cher
Tashi Döndrup	Bkra shis don grub
Tashi Gomang	Bkra shis sgo mang

Thelé	The le
Thöpa Gyatso	thos pa rgya mtsho
tishri	ti shrī
tönpa	ston pa
torma, tormas	gtor ma
tötsok	bstod tshogs
trikor	khri skor
Tri Ralpachen	Khri ral pa can
Trisong Detsen	Khri srong lde'u btsan
Tsalpa	Tshal pa
Tsanaidap	Tsha sna'i 'dab
Tsang Chumik Ringmo	Gtsang chu mig ring mo
Tsang Trompa	Gtsang gi grom pa
Tsangpai drukdra	tshangs pa'i 'brug sgra
Tsechen Kunchab Ling	brtse chen kun khyab gling
Üdepa Lopön Sangyé Bum	Dbus sde pa Slob dpon Sangs rgyas 'bum
Üpa Sangbum	Dbus pa Sangs 'bum
Ü-Tsang	dbus gtsang
Ütsé Nyingma	Dbu rtse rnying ma
Uyuk	'U yug
Uyukpa	'U yug pa
yanlak dunpai chöpa	yan lag bdun pa'i mchod pa
Yarlungpa Jangchup Gyaltsen	Yar lung pa Byang chub rgyal mtshan
yönten	yon tan
Yöntri	Yon khri

Glossary

absolute truth. Reality examined and determined to be beyond explanation, beyond words, beyond perception, beyond speech.

Abhidharma. One of the three divisions of the Tripiṭaka. A precise and exhaustive accounting of phenomenon.

Akaniṣṭha. The highest realm of subtle materiality.

anuttarayoga. Highest of the four different classes of tantra in Buddhism.

Āryan path. The path of application; it joins the worldly level to the beyond-worldly level.

arūpadhātu. The formless realm.

asaṃskṛtadharma. Unconditioned phenomena.

Avalokiteśvara. The bodhisattva of great compassion.

bardo being: A spirit with no physical body experiencing the period between death and rebirth.

bhikṣu (m.)/bhikṣuṇī (f.) vows. The highest level of ordination as a Buddhist monk or nun.

bhūmi. A stage of a bodhisattva's realization leading to buddhahood. The bhūmis, normally enumerated as ten, begin at the path of seeing and culminate in full enlightenment.

bodhicitta. See **enlightenment mind.**

bodhisattva. One who through great compassion has generated the resolution to attain enlightenment for the benefit of all beings.

Bodhisattvayāna. The way by which bodhisattvas practice to attain buddhahood, focused on the development of the six perfections.

Buddha Amitābha. The buddha of the Western pure land.

calm-abiding meditation. Or śamatha, in Sanskrit. The practice of focusing the mind single-pointedly without the interference of thoughts.

caryā. One of the four different classes of tantra in Buddhism.

creation and completion. The two stages of tantric practice.

dākinī. Female tantric helper deity.

defilement (klesha). Negative actions of body, voice, and mind, which cause suffering. The root defilement is ignorance, which conditions desire and hatred, and these three in turn drive all the others. Along with contaminated karma, defilements keep us locked in samsara.

Dharma. The Buddha's teachings and realizations. Lowercase *dharmas* means "phenomena."

dharmadhātu. "Sphere of reality"; the essence of phenomena, which is emptiness.

dharmakāya. "Body of reality"; one of the three bodies, or aspects, of a perfectly enlightened buddha. Can just refer to ultimate truth, a buddha's realization.

dharmatā. The ultimate reality.

eighteen prerequisites. Prerequisites necessary for a life in which it is possible to practice the Dharma. Such a life is known as a precious human birth. The prerequisites include freedom from eight unfavorable conditions and endowment with ten favorable conditions. See also eight freedoms; ten endowments

eight freedoms. Eight of the eighteen prerequisites of perfect human birth. The first four are freedom from the nonhuman states of birth as a hell being, a hungry ghost, an animal, or a long-lived god. Four are within the human realm, namely, freedom from birth among barbarians, birth among people with wrong beliefs, birth in a place where a buddha has not appeared, and birth as a person whose physical or mental impairment prevents their receiving the Dharma.

eight-limbed vows. Guidelines for living a wholesome life. They consist of three branches: the branch of moral conduct, which includes abstaining from killing, stealing, lying, and sexual activity; the branch of attentiveness, which consists of abstaining from intoxication; the branch of ascetic practices, which includes avoiding sitting on a high seat, abstaining from eating after midday, and abstaining from singing, dancing, and wearing jewels or cosmetics.

eight worldly dharmas. These eight are worldly mind-states given in four pairs: concerns for gain and loss, pleasure and pain, fame and disrepute, praise and blame.

enlightenment mind (bodhichitta). The resolve to attain enlightenment for the benefit of all sentient beings. Enlightenment mind may be divided into wishing enlightenment mind and entering enlightenment mind to refer to the phases of its development from aspiration to actual practice. Or it may be divided into relative enlightenment mind and ultimate enlightenment mind to refer, respectively, to the altruisic wish and to the realization of primordial wisdom free of elaboration.

entering enlightenment mind. Making a vow to engage in the practices to attain enlightenment for the benefit of all beings in a ritual before a spiritual preceptor, and undertaking the practice of the six perfections.

five dhyani buddhas. Each presents the five qualities of the Buddha.

five precepts. In Sanskrit, *pañcaśīla*. Abstain from killing, stealing; sexual activity, lying, and intoxication.

four major sufferings. Birth, old age, sickness, and death.

Gaṇapati. A wealth deity.

A Garland of Jewels. A collection of advice to the prince Gibek Timur, composed by Chögyal Phagpa.

A Gift of Dharma to Kublai Khan. A classic teaching composed by Chögyal Phagpa for Kublai Khan, explaining the Mahāyāna path with a special emphasis on the nature of mind and reality.

Heart Sūtra. A Mahāyāna Buddhist sūtra explaining the fundamental emptiness of all phenomena, known through and as the five aggregates of human existence: form, sensation, perception, thought process, consciousness.

Hevajra. A tutelary deity who is the integration of compassion and wisdom.

interdependent origination. The theory that all phenomena arise due to causes and conditions rather than existing inherently.

kalpa. A Sanskrit word meaning "eon."

kāmadhātu. The desire realm; the realm in which most sentient beings cycle through rebirths. It includes the three lower realms of hell beings, hungry ghosts, and animals and the three higher realms of humans, demigods, and some of the gods.

Kangyur. Literally "Translated Words"; the canon containing the 84,000 teachings of Tibetan Buddhism spoken by the Buddha. It includes sections on vinaya, sūtras, and tantras.

kāya. "Body" or aspect, especially of a buddha. The three kāyas, or three bodies of a buddha, are the dharmakāya, the saṃbhogakāya, and the nirmāṇakāya.

kriyā. One of the four classes of tantra in Buddhism.

Lamdré. Literally, "path and result"; the special instructions on the practice of Hevajra tantra unique to the Sakya tradition.

Madhyamaka. The Middle Way. A philosophical subschool of Mahayāna Buddhism that holds that the nature of all phenomena is characterized by neither the extreme of existence nor the extreme of nonexistence.

mahāmudrā. Literally "great seal"; realization of the ultimate nature of one's mind, its lack of inherent nature.

mahāparinirvāṇa. The end of an enlightened being's physical life.

mahāsiddha. A greatly accomplished meditator, often referring in particular to the early Indian masters in the tantric lineages.

Mahāvairocana. The central deity of the *Mahāvairocanābhisaṃbodhi Sūtra*.

Mahāyāna. "Great Vehicle"; one of the two major schools of Buddhism, the Mahāyāna emphasizes following the conduct and view of bodhisattvas, who strive for enlightenment to save all beings.

Mañjuśrī. The bodhisattva of wisdom.

Mantrayāna vow. Vows received by initiates in a Vajrayāna empowerment.

Middle Way. See Madhyamaka

muni. A holy, noble, or wise person. The Buddha is the highest muni.

Nālandā. A great Buddhist seat of learning in ancient India and the source of Tibetan Buddhism's dominant philosophical traditions.

Nāgārjuna. Considered to be one of the most important Mahāyāna philosophers and the founder of the Madhyamaka school of Mahāyāna Buddhism.

nirmāṇakāya. "Body of emanations"; one of the three bodies of a perfectly enlightened buddha. Typically refers to the human form emanated by a buddha in order to benefit beings.

nirvāṇa. Personal liberation; the cessation of suffering and its causes.

nonabiding nirvāṇa. The great nirvāṇa, which is above both saṃsāra and nirvāṇa; the state of buddhahood.

objectless meditation: The practice of resting in awareness of the flow of experiences without specifically attending to any of them.

pāramitā. Perfection. See **six perfections.**

Pāramitāyāna. The "Perfection Vehicle"; the sūtric practice of the gradual path of pursuing enlightenment primarily through the practices of refuge, enlightenment mind, and the six perfections.

parinirvāṇa. Final nirvāṇa; the release of the enlightened soul from the cycle of rebirth.

Parting from the Four Attachments. A cycle of teachings spoken by the bodhisattva Mañjuśrī to the Sakya master Sachen Kunga Nyingpo.

path of accumulation. The first of the five paths, or progressive levels of realization, leading to buddhahood. On this path the practitioner begins to intentionally accumulate merits.

path of application. The second of the five paths, or progressive levels of realization, leading to buddhahood. This is the joint or transition between the worldly and the beyond-worldly levels. On this path, realized practitioners experience signs that they are nearing realization of nonconceptual wisdom.

path of meditation. The fourth of the five paths, or progressive levels of realization, leading to buddhahood. The practitioner on this path meditates on the ultimate truth realized on the path of seeing, and abandons faults.

path of no-more-learning. The fifth and final of the five paths, or progressive levels of realization, leading to buddhahood. This is the level of buddhahood. At this stage, all obscurations to knowledge are eliminated and all perfections attained.

path of seeing. The third of the five paths, or progressive levels of realization, leading to buddhahood. On this path, a practitioner realizes the ultimate truth of the lack of inherent nature of phenomenon directly for the first time and enters the first bodhisattva bhūmi.

prajñāpāramitā. *The Perfection of Wisdom* scriptures, which teach the view of emptiness.

prakṛti. The transformation of primal nature.

pramāṇa. Literally, "proof": the means of acquiring true knowledge.

prātimokṣa. The individual liberation vows for purifying physical and verbal defilements.

pratyekabuddha. "Solitary realizer"; a Śrāvakayāna practitioner who attains nirvāṇa for himself alone without aid from a teacher in the life that he became a pratyekabuddha.

Pratyekabuddhayāna. The path of practice of a pratyekabuddha.

primordial wisdom. The basic nature of every sentient being's mind, which is empty of inherent nature and free of conceptual thought.

puruṣa. The notion of pure self.

refuge. The first vows on the Buddhist path. By promising to rely on the Buddha as the one who shows the path, the Dharma as the path, and the Sangha as one's companions on the path, one officially becomes a Buddhist.

relative truth. Reality to be as it appears in an unexamined way.

ringsel. Blessings that appear in the cremated remains of great masters.

rūpadhātu. The realm of forms; the first of the physical realms.

sādhana. A spiritual practice, such as prayer or meditation, with the goal to attain enlightenment.

Sakya Paṇḍita. The fourth of the five founders of the Sakya order and great sage of Tibet.

samādhi. Single-pointed concentration; meditation.

śamatha. Concentration meditation, also known as calm-abiding meditation.

samaya. Another name for the Vajrayāna vows, which guide the person following the tantric path.

saṃbhogakāya. "Body of enjoyment"; one of the three bodies of a perfectly enlightened buddha. Refers to a buddha's exalted form visible in the pure buddha fields and to highly realized beings.

saṃsāra. The cycle of suffering and rebirth fueled by defilements and karma.

saṃskṛtadharma. Conditioned phenomena.

Saṅgha. The community of followers of the Buddha, especially bodhisattvas who have reached the irreversible stage of the path.

siddhi. The temporary and ultimate accomplishments that are attained through spiritual practice.

Śiva. A Hindu deity.

six perfections. The Mahāyāna practices prescribed for a bodhisattva: the perfections of generosity, moral conduct, patience, effort, concentration, and wisdom.

śrāmaṇera. A monastic novice who holds ten vows.

śrāvaka. "Hearer" or "disciple"; a practitioner who attains personal liberation or nirvāṇa by relying on a teacher.

Śrāvakayāna. The paths of practice of a śravaka.

Sukhāvatī. The realm or buddha field of the red Buddha Amitābha.

śūnyatā. Emptiness.

supramundane path. Teachings on the paths of seeing, meditation, and no-more-learning.

svābhāvikakāya. The indivisible aspect of the three holy bodies of a buddha.

ten bodhisattva levels. See bhūmi

ten endowments. The ten endowments necessary for a life in which one can practice Dharma, five acquired by oneself and five acquired from others. The five acquired by oneself are birth: as a human, in a central realm, with sound sense organs, without having committed heinous crimes, and with sincere faith in the Buddha's teachings. The five acquired from others are birth at a time during which: a buddha has come into this world, a buddha has bestowed the teachings, the teachings continue to be upheld as a living tradition, the followers are practicing, and sponsors are supporting the Dharma.

three bodies of a buddha. See **kāya.**

Three Jewels. The Buddha, the Dharma, and the Saṅgha.

tishri. Teacher of the Mongolian emperor.

tönpa. A Tibetan word meaning "teacher" or "guide."

torma. A sculpture made mostly of flour and butter used in tantric rituals or as offerings in Tibetan Buddhism.

trikor. One group of ten thousand subjects. Within one trikor are four thousand religious communities and six thousand lay families.

Tripiṭaka. The traditional term for the Buddhist scriptures.

upāsaka. Buddhist layperson. A follower of Buddhism who is not a monk or nun but who undertakes the five precepts: to not kill, steal, lie, engage in sexual activity, or become intoxicated.

Triple Gem. See **Three Jewels.**

uṣṇīṣa. The three-dimensional oval on the top of the Buddha's head.

Ü-Tsang. One of the three traditional provinces of Tibet.

vajra. A Sanskrit term meaning "indestructible." It refers to the ultimate wisdom of emptiness. Also, a ritual implement held in tantric practice and commonly depicted in Buddhist iconography.

Vajradhara. The ultimate primordial Buddha.

Vajradhātu. The realm of ultimate reality.

Vajrapāṇi. A bodhisattva who manifests spiritual power. He wields a vajra in his right hand.

Vajrayāna. The tantric path.

vidarśanā. Meditative insight.

vidyādhara. A master who constantly abides in the state of pure awareness.

vinaya. The portion of the Buddhist canon that deals with morality and discipline.

vipaśyanā. Insight wisdom, or the meditation to develop the realization of ultimate truth.

vīra. Male tantric helper deity.

Viṣṇu. A powerful worldly Hindu deity.

wishing enlightenment mind. Arousing the aspiration to attain perfect enlightenment for the benefit of all beings.

yogi. An ascetic practitioner of meditation.

Illustration Credits

Image 2 of the color insert:
Sakya Paṇḍita (1182–1251) and Chögyal Phagpa (1235–1280) with Mahākāla Lineage Masters
Central Tibet; 17th–18th century
Pigments on cloth
Rubin Museum of Art
Gift of Shelley and Donald Rubin
C2006.66.23 (HAR 695)

Image 3 of the color insert:
Lama (Teacher), Chögyal Phagpa
Tibet; 16th century
Pigments on cloth
Rubin Museum of Art
C2002.3.2 (HAR 65046)

Image 4 of the color insert:
Courtesy of Ani Jhampa Nyima.

About the Author

His Holiness Kyabgon Gongma Sakya Trichen Rinpoche is the Forty-First Sakya Trizin, the previous throne holder of the Sakya Lineage of Tibetan Buddhism. His religious name is Ngawang Kunga Tegchen Palbar Trinley Samphel Wangyi Gyalpo. He passed the throne of the Sakya lineage to his elder son Ratna Vajra Rinpoche who became the Forty-Second Sakya Trizin on March 9, 2017. He is considered second only to the Dalai Lama in the spiritual hierarchy of Tibetan Buddhism. In the year 2001, His Holiness established Tsechen Kunchab Ling in Walden, New York, as the seat of the Sakya Trizins of the Dolma Phodrang in the United States, and appointed Venerable Khenpo Kalsang Gyaltsen as abbot. He is the author of *Freeing the Heart and Mind: Part One, Introduction to the Buddhist Path.*

What to Read Next from Wisdom Publications

Freeing the Heart and Mind
Part One: Introduction to the Buddhist Path
His Holiness the Sakya Trichen

The first book by His Holiness the Sakya Trichen, it includes an introduction to Buddhism and commentary from His Holiness on important Sakya texts.

The Sakya School of Tibetan Buddhim
A History
Dhongthog Rinpoche
Translated by Sam Van Schaik

Explore a complete history of one of Tibet's four main Buddhist schools, from its origins to the present day.

Luminous Lives
The Story of the Early Masters of the Lam 'bras Tradition in Tibet
Cyrus Stearns

"A seminal manuscript history of its earliest practitioners and masters, and a detailed description of the Lam 'bras teachings."—*Tricycle*

Ordinary Wisdom
Sakya Pandita's Treasury of Good Advice
John Davenport
Foreword by His Holiness the Sakya Trichen

"A sterling translation of one of the most loved books of the Tibetan Buddhist tradition."—Gehlek Rinpoche

Freedom from Extremes
Gorampa's "Distinguishing the Views" and the Polemics of Emptiness
José I. Cabezón
Geshe Lobsang Dargyay

"A magnificent translation of a pivotal Tibetan examination of the nature of reality. Essential for comprehending the variety of views on the middle ground."—Jeffrey Hopkins, University of Virginia

About Wisdom Publications

Wisdom Publications is the leading publisher of classic and contemporary Buddhist books and practical works on mindfulness. To learn more about us or to explore our other books, please visit our website at wisdompubs.org or contact us at the address below.

Wisdom Publications
199 Elm Street
Somerville, MA 02144 USA

We are a 501(c)(3) organization, and donations in support of our mission are tax deductible.

Wisdom Publications is affiliated with the Foundation for the Preservation of the Mahayana Tradition (FPMT).